Land Patent Guide

A Practical Guide to Understanding What Land Patents Really Are, How They Relate to Modern Property Law, and How Homeowners Can Evaluate Their Relevance Without Legal Guesswork

Gilbert Hodgson

IMPORTANT NOTICE — LIMITATION OF LIABILITY

This book is published solely for informational and educational purposes. It does not constitute legal, tax, financial, or professional advice of any kind. The author is not a licensed attorney and nothing in this text should be construed as the practice of law.

The information contained herein reflects the author's understanding as of the date of publication and may not account for subsequent changes in statutes, regulations, administrative rules, or judicial interpretations. Real property law in the United States varies significantly from state to state, and often from county to county. No general-purpose resource can substitute for the analysis of a specific situation by a qualified professional. Any reader who intends to take legal, tax, or administrative action regarding real property is strongly encouraged to consult a licensed attorney in the relevant jurisdiction before acting.

The author and publisher disclaim all liability for damages of any kind — direct, indirect, incidental, consequential, or otherwise — arising from the use or inability to use the information contained in this book.

All trademarks referenced in this book are the property of their respective owners and are used solely for identification and descriptive purposes. Their use does not imply any affiliation with or endorsement by the trademark holders.

Statutory references, judicial opinions, and online resources cited in this book are provided to assist the reader's independent research and do not constitute an exhaustive survey of applicable law.

Table Of Contents

Introduction

The Gap Between Online Claims and Legal Reality

Few subjects in the modern property landscape generate as much confident certainty and simultaneous confusion as land patents. A homeowner searching for answers online can, within minutes, encounter videos, articles, forum posts, and downloadable documents that claim to unlock a deeper truth about ownership—one that courts, banks, and governments supposedly ignore or suppress. The language used is often persuasive, sometimes urgent, and almost always absolute. According to these claims, the solution to insecurity, taxation, foreclosure, or legal vulnerability lies in rediscovering an old instrument and asserting it with enough conviction.

What rarely accompanies these declarations is a careful explanation of how modern property systems actually function, how authority is distributed among federal, state, and local institutions, or how courts interpret claims that rest on historical documents in contemporary disputes. The result is a widening gap between what is promised in online spaces and what is recognized in legal reality. That gap is not merely academic. It affects real decisions, real property, and real families.

The digital environment rewards certainty far more than nuance. A video titled with a bold claim spreads more quickly than a measured explanation. A simplified narrative is easier to absorb than a layered one. Over time, this creates a distorted picture in which complexity is framed as deception and restraint is mistaken for ignorance or fear.

The problem is not that people are curious about land patents. Curiosity is rational.

The problem arises when curiosity is met with information that collapses centuries of legal development into slogans, treating modern courts as irrelevant obstacles rather than governing authorities. To understand why this matters, a few facts help set the stage. The General Land Office was established by Congress in 1812 under 2 Stat. 716 to manage the orderly disposition of public lands. Between 1812 and 1946, when the GLO was folded into the newly created Bureau of Land Management, the federal government issued more than two million land patents, transferring land from the public domain into private ownership across thirty states.

These records are preserved today in the BLM's General Land Office Records database (glorecords.blm.gov), freely accessible to anyone with an internet connection.

That history is real, and it matters.

But property law in the United States is not static. It did not freeze at the moment a patent was issued, nor did it stop evolving once land passed from federal disposition into private hands. Legal systems adapt through statutes, case law, administrative practice, and recorded procedures. The Supreme Court recognized this as early as 1839, when it held in Wilcox v. Jackson, 38 U.S. 498, that once title passes from the United States under federal law, "that property, like all other property in the state, is subject to state legislation. "Ignoring that evolution does not restore an earlier reality; it creates a fictional one. Many online claims rely on selective citations, historical fragments taken out of context, or misunderstandings of how supremacy, jurisdiction, and recording systems operate today. This disconnect is especially dangerous because it presents itself as empowerment. It suggests that homeowners are one document away from reclaiming control, one filing away from overturning layers of law. Yet empowerment built on incomplete or inaccurate premises often leads not to security, but to exposure. When expectations shaped online collide with institutional reality, the consequences are rarely theoretical. They appear as rejected filings, dismissed arguments, increased scrutiny, or irreversible legal missteps. In one notable example, a petitioner who invoked land patent theories and sovereign citizen doctrines in a 2019 filing to the U.S. Supreme Court (Docket No. 18-8013) saw the petition denied without discussion — an outcome consistent with decades of judicial treatment of such arguments.

The challenge, then, is not deciding whether land patents matter. The challenge is understanding how claims about them are constructed, what they omit, and how far removed they are from the systems that actually govern property today. Closing that gap requires patience, historical literacy, and a willingness to accept that reality is often less dramatic, but far more reliable, than the stories told about it.

This tension between promise and practice sets the stage for a deeper question, one that many homeowners struggle to articulate but feel acutely. If the information landscape is so fragmented, and if ownership is so often described in conflicting ways, what exactly does it mean to own property at all?

Why Homeowners Feel Uncertain About What They Truly Own

For most homeowners, ownership feels intuitive rather than technical. A home is purchased, documents are signed, keys are exchanged, and life continues.

Bills arrive, taxes are paid, repairs are made. For years, sometimes decades, nothing challenges the underlying assumption that the property is firmly and fully "owned." That sense of stability, however, often rests on a limited understanding of how ownership is defined, documented, and enforced.

Uncertainty tends to surface not in everyday life, but at moments of stress. A refinancing application raises unfamiliar terminology. A property tax notice arrives with language that feels less like ownership and more like obligation. A legal dispute in the neighborhood sparks questions about boundaries, easements, or authority. At that point, homeowners often realize that what they believed to be simple is layered with conditions, limitations, and external interests. This uncertainty is compounded by the way property concepts are discussed publicly.

Terms like "title," "deed," "ownership," and "rights" are used interchangeably in casual conversation, even though they carry distinct meanings in legal contexts.

A deed, for instance, is a conveyance instrument it documents a transfer. Title is the legal condition of ownership, shaped by the full history of recorded interests. A mortgage does not eliminate ownership; it creates a security interest held by the lender.

Without clear distinctions, it becomes difficult to assess what is actually held versus what is merely assumed.

When alternative explanations enter the picture, particularly those suggesting that conventional ownership is incomplete or illusory, the confusion deepens.

There is also an emotional dimension to this uncertainty. A home is not just an asset; it is shelter, stability, and legacy. When people encounter claims implying that their connection to that asset is weaker than they thought, anxiety naturally follows. That anxiety can push individuals toward explanations that promise certainty, even if those explanations oversimplify or distort reality. The desire for control, especially later in life or after years of financial effort, is powerful. Complicating matters further is the absence of accessible, neutral explanations.

Much of the available information is either highly technical or highly ideological. Legal textbooks are not written for homeowners, while activist narratives are not written with legal accountability in mind. The middle ground—clear, responsible discussion that acknowledges both historical foundations and modern frameworks—is surprisingly rare. As a result, homeowners are often left piecing together fragments. They may understand that a mortgage involves a lender's interest, but not how that interest is structured and the answer depends partly on whether they live in a title-theory state, where the lender holds legal title during repayment, or alien-theory state, where the borrower retains title and the lender holds only a security interest. They may know that taxes are assessed annually, but not why taxation persists regardless of how long the property has been held. Into that partial understanding enter claims that suggest a single overlooked mechanism explains everything. Without a stable reference point, it becomes difficult to evaluate such claims critically. This sense of uncertainty is not a failure of intelligence or diligence. It is the predictable outcome of a system that is complex by design and poorly explained in everyday language. Recognizing that complexity, rather than denying it, is the first step toward clarity. Once that recognition takes hold, the next question becomes practical rather than emotional: what kind of guidance is actually useful in navigating this landscape?

What This Guide Will and Will Not Do

The purpose of this guide is grounded in restraint rather than revelation. It does not promise to overturn established systems, invalidate governing institutions, or unlock hidden powers. Those promises are easy to make and difficult to defend. Instead, the focus here is on providing a clear lens through which claims about land patents and ownership can be evaluated without speculation or fear. This work is designed to support informed judgment. That means offering context where claims are often presented without it, and precision where language is frequently stretched beyond its legal meaning.

It means respecting historical documents without treating them as timeless trump cards, and acknowledging modern legal structures without portraying them as arbitrary or illegitimate.

Above all, it means prioritizing understanding over action for its own sake. Where relevant, this guide provides specific references, to federal and state statutes, judicial opinions, and publicly accessible databases, so that readers can verify claims independently rather than relying on any single source, including this one.

A glossary of legal terms and a set of appendices with statutory references, case law summaries, and research resources appear at the end of this book for that purpose.

Equally important is what this guide does not attempt to do. It does not function as a substitute for professional legal counsel, nor does it encourage readers to engage in filings or assertions based solely on written explanations. Legal systems are case-specific, fact-dependent, and influenced by jurisdictional nuances that no general resource can fully anticipate.

Property law varies not only from state to state, but often from county to county. What holds true in a public-domain state like Ohio may not apply in a state-land state like Texas or Pennsylvania, where land never passed through federal ownership at all.

Suggesting otherwise would be irresponsible.

This guide also avoids framing property ownership as a battle between individuals and institutions.

That framing may be emotionally compelling, but it obscures the reality that property law exists precisely to create predictability and order among competing interests.

Understanding those interests, rather than rejecting them outright, is what allows property owners to make decisions that hold up under scrutiny.

Readers should not expect simplified heroes or villains, nor should they expect guarantees.

What they should expect is a careful examination of how land patents are situated within a broader legal environment, how claims about them are constructed, and how those claims can be assessed without either cynicism or blind acceptance.

The goal is confidence rooted in comprehension, not confidence borrowed from rhetoric.

As the discussion progresses, attention remains firmly on the homeowner as a decision-maker, not as a crusader.

Decisions about property affect families, finances, and long-term security.

Approaching those decisions with patience and clarity is not a sign of weakness; it is a form of stewardship.

Chapter 1 – What Property Ownership Really Means in the United States

Ownership vs Possession vs Control

In everyday language, ownership is often treated as a simple idea. A person buys a house, moves in, and refers to it as "my property." The phrase feels complete, final, and self-explanatory.

Yet in legal reality, ownership is not a single condition but a relationship—one that exists alongside other relationships involving use, authority, obligation, and limitation.

Confusion begins when these different dimensions are collapsed into one word and assumed to mean the same thing in all contexts. Possession is the most visible of these dimensions. It refers to physical occupancy or use.

A homeowner who lives in a house possesses it in the most immediate sense. Keys are held, doors are locked, utilities are paid, and daily life unfolds within its walls. Possession is tangible and intuitive, which is why many people unconsciously equate it with ownership. However, possession alone does not determine legal standing. Renters possess property without owning it. Squatters may possess property unlawfully. Even owners can temporarily lose possession through lease agreements or court orders while retaining other legal interests.

Control operates on a different axis. It refers to decision-making authority—what can be done with the property, how it can be altered, and under what conditions it can be transferred or encumbered. Control is exercised through permissions and restrictions, many of which exist independently of physical presence. Zoning regulations, building codes, easements, and environmental rules all shape control without removing possession. A homeowner may fully occupy a property while being unable to build, subdivide, or modify it in certain ways. Control, therefore, is distributed rather than absolute.

Ownership, as recognized in U.S. law, sits at the intersection of these concepts but does not collapse into any one of them. Legal ownership is a bundle of recognized interests acknowledged by governing authority and enforced through courts. It includes rights to use, exclude, transfer, and benefit from property, but each of those rights is subject to conditions.

The U.S. Supreme Court has described these components in several landmark decisions. In Kaiser Aetna v. United States, 444 U.S. 164 (1979), the Court identified the right to exclude others as "one of the most essential sticks in the bundle of rights that are commonly characterized as property. "Ownership does not eliminate external authority; it exists within a framework that defines its scope.

This distinction becomes especially important when property is discussed as though it were immune from limitation. Many popular narratives frame ownership as something that can be fully reclaimed or restored, as if modern constraints were optional overlays rather than foundational components of the system. That framing misunderstands how property law developed in the United States. From its earliest days, property ownership existed within a legal order designed to balance individual interests with collective governance. The idea of property as entirely detached from obligation has never been operative in practice.

Consider the difference between holding title to land and exercising unrestricted authority over it. Title signifies recognition by the legal system that a particular interest exists. It does not guarantee that every desired use will be permitted, nor does it insulate the owner from taxation, regulation, or dispute. The
Fifth Amendment to the U.S. Constitution acknowledges this directly: it does not prohibit the government from taking private property, but requires that "just compensation" be paid when it does.

The Takings Clause, as interpreted in cases from Pennsylvania Coal Co. v. Mahon, 260 U.S. 393 (1922)through Sheetz v. County of El Dorado (2024), establishes that even regulatory actions can constitute a taking if they go too far but the existence of the clause itself confirms that ownership operates within, not above, constitutional governance.
Ownership confers standing, not supremacy. It grants the right to participate in the legal system as an owner, not the right to operate outside that system.

The tendency to blur ownership with control often leads to misplaced expectations. When homeowners encounter limitations—whether financial, regulatory, or procedural—they may feel that ownership has been compromised or undermined. In reality, what they are encountering is the normal operation of a system in which ownership has always been conditional, contextual, and relational. The law does not promise isolation; it promises recognition.

Understanding this distinction does not weaken ownership. It clarifies it. Once ownership is understood as a legally recognized position rather than a claim of independence, it becomes easier to assess what protections exist and where boundaries lie. Possession explains who occupies. Control explains who decides. Ownership explains who is recognized.

That recognition, however, is not granted in a vacuum. It is expressed through documents, recorded interests, and enforceable agreements that together form the structure through which ownership is identified and maintained. To understand how ownership functions in practice, it is necessary to look more closely at the instruments through which it is defined.

Deeds, Titles, Mortgages, and Recorded Interests Explained

Property ownership in the United States is not proven by declaration or belief. It is established through documentation that records how interests in land are created, transferred, and encumbered over time. These records are not merely bureaucratic artifacts; they are the backbone of the system that allows ownership to be recognized, contested, and enforced. Misunderstanding how these instruments work is one of the most common sources of confusion surrounding property rights. A deed is often mistaken for ownership itself. In reality, a deed is a conveyance document. It records the transfer of an interest from one party to another. Its function is transactional rather than declarative. When properly executed and recorded, it provides evidence that a transfer occurred, but it does not stand alone. A deed's meaning depends on the validity of the interest being conveyed and the context in which it is recorded. Not all deeds are equal. A general warranty deed provides the strongest protection, with the grantor guaranteeing clear title against all prior claims. A special warranty deed limits that guarantee to the period of the grantor's ownership.

A quitclaim deed offers no warranty at all, it merely transfers whatever interest the grantor may hold, if any. In Beard v. Federy, 70 U.S. 478 (1865), the U.S. Supreme Court described the operation of a land patent itself as essentially that of a quitclaim, a conveyance of whatever interest the United States possessed in the land. Title, by contrast, is not a single document. It is a concept that refers to the legal status of ownership as established by the accumulation of recorded interests. Title represents the condition of ownership as it exists at a given moment, shaped by past transfers, liens, restrictions, and claims. When people speak of "holding title," they are referring to the legal recognition of their interest within this broader historical record. Mortgages add another layer to this structure. Contrary to common assumption, a mortgage does not negate ownership. It creates a security interest in favor of a lender, tying repayment obligations to the property. Depending on jurisdiction, the legal mechanics vary, but the effect is consistent: the property becomes collateral. Ownership continues to exist, but it is burdened by an enforceable claim. This claim does not erase ownership; it qualifies it. How the mortgage is structured depends on state law. In roughly twenty "title theory" states, including Georgia, Massachusetts, Maryland, and North Carolina, the lender holds legal title to the property until the loan is repaid. In the approximately thirty "lien theory" states — including California, New York, Florida, and Illinois — the borrower retains title and the lender holds only a security interest (a lien). A handful of states, such as Ohio and New Jersey, follow an intermediary approach in which the lender acquires title only upon default. The practical differences matter most when disputes arise over foreclosure procedures or the borrower's rights during repayment.

Recorded interests extend beyond deeds and mortgages. Easements grant use rights to others.

Covenants impose conditions on use. Liens secure obligations unrelated to purchase financing. Each of these interests is recorded to provide notice and establish priority. Recording does not create the interest, but it makes it enforceable against third parties. The public record functions as a shared reference point, allowing all participants to assess the condition of a property before acquiring an interest in it.

The recording system is often misunderstood as optional or secondary. In practice, it is central. Courts rely on recorded instruments to resolve disputes, determine priority, and assess good faith. An interest that exists only in theory, without proper documentation or notice, carries little weight when challenged. This is why property law places such emphasis on recordation rather than assertion. The specific rules governing how recording determines priority vary by state. Under a "race" statute, the first party to record prevails regardless of knowledge. Under a "notice" statute, the last good-faith purchaser without notice of a prior claim prevails. Under a "race-notice" statute, the most common type, used in approximately thirty states including California, New York, and Colorado, a party must both lack notice of the prior claim and record first. These distinctions carry real consequences when competing interests collide, and they apply to all recorded instruments, including those referencing land patents.

Confusion arises when documents are treated as symbols rather than tools. A deed is not a talisman. A mortgage is not an illusion. Recorded interests are not conspiratorial impositions. They are mechanisms designed to balance competing claims in a way that can be publicly verified. When homeowners encounter alternative narratives suggesting that these mechanisms are invalid or irrelevant, they are often being invited to disregard the very system that protects their recognized interests.

Understanding these instruments requires abandoning the search for a single, definitive document that proves everything. Ownership is evidenced through coherence, not isolation. A clean title is not clean because it rests on one paper, but because its recorded history is consistent, complete, and uncontested. Breaks in that coherence create risk, regardless of how strongly ownership is asserted.

As these layers accumulate, they form a structure that is sometimes described as complex or opaque. Yet that complexity serves a purpose. It allows property to be transferred, financed, inherited, and regulated without resorting to force or personal authority. It replaces conflict with procedure. To appreciate that structure fully, one must accept that ownership is not a binary state, but a composite one.

Why Property Ownership Is Layered, Not Absolute

The idea of absolute ownership is emotionally appealing. It suggests permanence, autonomy, and immunity from interference. In practice, however, property ownership in the United States has never operated on that basis. Instead, it functions as a layered arrangement of rights and obligations, each recognized within a broader legal order. This layered structure is not a flaw; it is the mechanism that allows property to exist as a stable institution rather than a contested prize.

At its core, layering reflects the reality that land cannot exist in isolation. Every parcel sits within a jurisdiction, relies on shared infrastructure, and affects neighboring interests. Roads cross boundaries. Utilities connect multiple properties. Environmental impacts do not respect lot lines. Absolute ownership would make coordinated use impossible. Layered ownership makes coexistence manageable.

These layers take many forms. Some arise from voluntary agreements, such as financing arrangements or shared access rights. Others are imposed through law, such as taxation or safety regulations. Still others emerge from historical conditions that continue to shape present use.

What unites them is that none negate ownership; they define its contours.

The mistake many people make is assuming that the presence of limits indicates the absence of ownership. This assumption misunderstands how rights function. Rights are meaningful precisely because they are defined. An undefined right is unenforceable. By specifying where authority begins and ends, the law transforms abstract claims into actionable positions. Ownership gains strength through recognition, not through denial of structure. American property law has long recognized four inherent limitations on private ownership, sometimes called the four powers of government over real property. Taxation allows government to assess and collect revenue based on property value. Eminent domain permits the taking of private property for public use upon payment of just compensation, as governed by the Fifth Amendment and applied to the states through the Fourteenth.

Police power authorizes regulation for the public health, safety, and welfare — the constitutional basis for zoning, upheld in Village of Euclid v. Ambler Realty Co., 272 U.S. 365 (1926). And escheat provides that property reverts to the state when an owner dies without heirs or a valid will. These four powers exist regardless of how ownership originated. They apply to land conveyed by patent no differently than to land acquired by deed last week. No instrument of conveyance, however old or however worded, exempts property from these powers.

Layering also explains why ownership can feel secure most of the time and uncertain at specific moments. When interests align—when obligations are met, records are clear, and use is uncontroversial—layers remain invisible. When conflict arises, those same layers become visible as they determine whose interest prevails. This visibility is often mistaken for intrusion, when it is actually resolution.

Another source of misunderstanding lies in the assumption that older claims are inherently stronger than newer ones. Historical priority matters, but it does not override subsequent legal developments. The law does not treat time as a freeze-frame. It incorporates history into a living system, one that continuously reconciles past actions with present governance. Ownership persists through that reconciliation, not outside it.

Recognizing ownership as layered encourages a more accurate form of confidence. Instead of relying on absolute claims that fail under scrutiny, it allows homeowners to assess where their position is strongest and where it is qualified. That assessment is not a concession; it is an exercise of responsibility.

Knowing how interests stack, overlap, and interact is what allows ownership to be defended effectively.

Layered ownership also clarifies why attempts to simplify property law often backfire. Removing layers does not restore freedom; it removes protection. The same recording requirements that feel restrictive also prevent secret claims. The same regulatory frameworks that impose conditions also create predictability. Ownership without layers would be ownership without stability.

Where Land Patents Fit Within the Modern Ownership Framework

Once ownership is understood as layered rather than absolute, the question of where land patents belong becomes far less dramatic—and far more precise.

Much of the confusion surrounding land patents stems from treating them as something external to the modern property system, as if they operate on a separate plane, immune to the structures described earlier.

In reality, land patents are not outside the framework of property ownership in the United States. They are embedded within it, historically foundational yet functionally limited by the same mechanisms that govern all recognized interests today.

A land patent is best understood as an origin point, not an operating authority. It represents the moment at which land passed from sovereign control into private hands under federal authority. That moment matters historically and legally, but it does not suspend time.

Once land enters private ownership, it becomes subject to the evolving legal environment that governs all private property.

The patent establishes the first recognized private interest; it does not freeze the rules that apply thereafter.

This distinction is crucial. Many contemporary claims treat land patents as if they retain an active, overriding power capable of nullifying subsequent layers of law. That interpretation misunderstands how legal continuity works.

Property systems do not operate on the principle that the earliest document always dominates later ones. They operate on the principle that interests accumulate, interact, and are interpreted within the current legal context.

The Supreme Court made this explicit in Wilcox v. Jackson, 38 U.S. 498 (1839): once land title passes under federal law, that property becomes subject to state legislation "so far as that legislation is consistent with the admission that the title passed and vested according to the laws of the United States".

A land patent does not sit above that context; it sits within the historical record that informs it. Modern ownership relies on recognition, enforceability, and predictability.

Courts, recording offices, and administrative bodies function based on present-day statutes and precedents. While historical instruments are acknowledged, they are interpreted through contemporary legal standards.

A land patent may establish that land was once part of the public domain and lawfully conveyed, but it does not provide an independent mechanism for bypassing current obligations or authorities.

This is where expectations often diverge from reality. The language used in patents—formal, declarative, and authoritative—can give the impression of permanence without limitation.

Yet permanence of origin is not the same as permanence of effect. The legal system does not treat patents as living commands; it treats them as completed acts. Their role is evidentiary, not operational. They explain how ownership began, not how it must be exercised indefinitely. As one early Ohio court put it in Roads v. Symmes, 1 Ohio 281, 314 (1824): "The patent is not the foundation, but the consummation of the title. Until it emanates, the legal power of the government over the subject is not at an end." Once it does emanate, that power terminates — and the land enters the ordinary stream of private ownership.

Within the modern framework, land patents function as part of the chain of recognized interests.

They can be relevant when tracing origin, resolving historical ambiguities, or confirming that land was properly conveyed out of federal ownership.

They do not function as tools for redefining ownership once that chain has developed through subsequent transfers, encumbrances, and regulations. Attempting to elevate them beyond that role often creates friction with the very institutions that determine property outcomes.

Another source of misunderstanding lies in conflating symbolic authority with legal authority.

Land patents carry symbolic weight because they are associated with sovereignty, original disposition, and foundational acts of government.

Symbolism, however, does not equate to legal leverage. Courts do not enforce symbolism; they enforce recognized interests as defined by current law.

When land patents are presented as symbols of ultimate control rather than as historical instruments, they are stripped of their actual legal function and replaced with expectations they cannot fulfill.

Understanding where land patents fit also requires acknowledging the role of jurisdiction. Property law in the United States is largely administered at the state and local level.

While federal actions initiate certain aspects of ownership, day-to-day governance—taxation, zoning, enforcement, dispute resolution—operates within state-defined systems.

The federal government's power to dispose of public lands derives from the Property Clause of the Constitution, Article IV, Section 3, Clause 2.

That power is exercised through conveyance — including patents — but it does not create a continuing federal jurisdiction over the land once conveyed.

A land patent does not relocate property into a separate jurisdiction. It does not remove it from the reach of the authorities that govern all private land within a state's borders.

This does not render land patents meaningless. It places them in proportion. They matter insofar as they contribute to clarity about origin and legitimacy of conveyance. They lose relevance when treated as instruments of exemption.

Modern ownership depends not on asserting distance from the system, but on navigating it competently. Instruments that align with that navigation retain value; those that attempt to bypass it tend to create vulnerability.

Another important aspect of fit is enforceability. An interest, regardless of its historical pedigree, must be enforceable to matter in practice. Enforceability depends on recognition by courts and administrative bodies.

Land patents are recognized as historical documents. They are not recognized as self-executing shields against obligations that arise later.

When homeowners are encouraged to treat patents as active defenses rather than contextual evidence, they are often being steered toward actions that lack enforceable support.

Seeing land patents in their proper place also reframes the emotional charge that often surrounds them.

Instead of representing a lost power waiting to be reclaimed, they represent a documented transition that allowed private ownership to exist in the first place.

That transition succeeded precisely because it was followed by systems of recording, transfer, and regulation. Without those systems, ownership would not have stabilized.

The patent did not replace structure; it enabled it.

For homeowners seeking clarity, this perspective offers something more valuable than dramatic promises.

It offers alignment with reality. Understanding that land patents sit at the foundation rather than the pinnacle of ownership allows decisions to be made without antagonism toward the institutions that actually determine outcomes.

It replaces confrontation with comprehension.

Within the modern ownership framework, land patents are neither magic keys nor irrelevant relics.

They are fixed reference points within a living system.

Their relevance depends on context, purpose, and expectations. When approached with restraint and understanding, they can inform knowledge. When approached as tools of override, they tend to generate conflict and disappointment.

Chapter 2 – What a Land Patent Actually Is (and What It Is Not)

The Legal Definition of a Land Patent in Plain English

A land patent is one of those legal terms that sounds self-explanatory until it is examined closely.

The word "patent" suggests exclusivity or authority, while "land" implies physical territory. Combined, they seem to promise a definitive form of ownership—something original, complete, and unchallengeable.

That impression is reinforced by the formal language used in historical patents, which often reads with a tone of finality. Yet the legal meaning of a land patent is both more modest and more precise than popular narratives suggest.

In plain terms, a land patent is the instrument by which a sovereign authority transfers land from public ownership into private hands. In the United States, this typically refers to the federal government's conveyance of public domain land to individuals, railroads, states, or other entities during periods of territorial expansion and settlement. The patent marks the point at which land ceases to be owned by the government and becomes subject to private ownership under law.

In legal terminology, a land patent is a form of "letters patent" — an open document issued under governmental seal that grants a right or status.

Black's Law Dictionary defines it as the instrument by which the government conveys a grant of public land to a private party. Unlike intellectual property patents, which expire, a land patent is permanent as to the fact of conveyance: it cannot be revoked except through a direct action by the government proving fraud in its procurement.

That description may sound straightforward, but its implications are often misunderstood. A land patent does not describe how land will be governed forever. It does not define the future rights, obligations, or immunities attached to that land. It documents a transaction, not a perpetual status.

The authority of a patent lies in its role as evidence of lawful conveyance, not as a standing source of power.

Legally, a land patent functions as a root of title. It establishes the first private link in the chain of ownership. From that point forward, ownership evolves through subsequent transfers, encumbrances, and legal developments.

The patent does not sit above those later events. It sits beneath them, supporting the legitimacy of the chain without controlling its direction.

One of the most persistent errors surrounding land patents is the assumption that their federal origin grants them a continuing supremacy. This assumption often rests on a misunderstanding of how federal authority operates.

The federal government's power to convey land does not imply a continuing federal interest in that land once the conveyance is complete. After transfer, governance shifts to the legal framework that applies to all privately held property within the relevant jurisdiction.

The language used in patents can be misleading to modern readers. Phrases that sound absolute were common in legal drafting of earlier eras, when formality was equated with clarity. Today, such language is often interpreted through a contemporary lens, leading readers to assign meanings that were never intended. Legal documents do not carry their authority through tone; they carry it through context and interpretation.

A land patent is not a license, nor is it a charter. It does not authorize the holder to act outside the law. It does not grant immunity from regulation, taxation, or dispute. Its legal force is confined to what it records: the lawful transfer of land at a specific moment in time. Everything that follows that moment is governed by the legal environment in which the land now exists.

Understanding this definition requires letting go of the idea that legal instruments operate as symbols of power.

They operate as records of authority exercised within a system. The patent records an exercise of authority that has already occurred. It does not project authority forward indefinitely.

When stripped of myth and restored to its legal role, the land patent becomes easier to understand and less susceptible to exaggeration. It is a foundational document, not a master key. It establishes legitimacy without dictating destiny. That clarity is essential, because confusion about what a patent is often bleeds into confusion about why it was created in the first place.

Original Purpose vs Modern Interpretation

To understand how land patents are interpreted today, it helps to step back and consider why they existed at all. Their original purpose was administrative, not philosophical.

Governments issued land patents to formalize settlement, encourage development, and establish orderly transfer of land from public control to private use.

They were tools of expansion, not statements of individual sovereignty.

In early America, vast tracts of land were held by the federal government.

Disposing of that land required a standardized method to ensure clarity, prevent overlapping claims, and legitimize ownership. Land patents served that function.

They were the endpoint of a process that included surveys, applications, compliance with statutory requirements, and official approval.

Once issued, the government's role in that particular parcel ended. The process was governed by a succession of federal statutes, each tailored to different circumstances and policy goals.

The Land Ordinance of 1785 and the Northwest Ordinance of 1787 established the survey grid and the principle of orderly disposition. The Homestead Act of 1862 (12 Stat. 392) allowed settlers to claim 160 acres of public land by living on it and cultivating it for five years. The Mining Law of 1872 (30 U.S.C. §§ 22–54) authorized patents for mining claims. The Desert Land Act of 1877 (43 U.S.C. § 321 et seq.) targeted arid lands in the West.

The Timber Culture Act of 1873 encouraged tree planting. The Stock Raising Homestead Act of 1916 addressed grazing lands but — critically — reserved all mineral rights to the United States in its Section 9. Each statute produced patents with different terms and conditions.

There was never a single, uniform "land patent"; there were many varieties, and the specific law under which a patent was issued determines what it actually conveyed.

Nothing in that process suggested that patents were intended to function as shields against future law. They were designed to integrate land into a legal system, not to isolate it from one.

The goal was stability, not exception.

Private ownership only made sense if it could be regulated, transferred, taxed, and inherited in predictable ways. Modern interpretations often diverge sharply from this historical reality. Some narratives treat land patents as if they embody an original contract that supersedes all later developments.

This interpretation assumes that law operates like a frozen agreement rather than a living system. In practice, law evolves precisely because circumstances change. Infrastructure expands, populations grow, and governance adapts. Property law reflects those changes.

The shift from original purpose to modern myth often occurs through selective reading. Passages from historical documents are extracted and presented without context.

Judicial opinions are cited without acknowledging the specific issues they addressed. The complexity of legal reasoning is flattened into declarative statements that sound authoritative but lack practical grounding.

Modern courts do not ignore land patents.

They recognize them as part of the historical record. However, recognition is not the same as deference.

Courts interpret patents within the framework of current law, not as standalone authorities. When patents are raised in disputes, they are evaluated for relevance, not reverence.

This distinction matters because modern property disputes are resolved based on present obligations and recognized interests. Taxes are assessed under current statutes. Zoning is enforced under current ordinances. Disputes are adjudicated under current procedural rules. A historical document may inform a court's understanding of how ownership began, but it does not dictate how ownership operates now. T

he federal government itself acknowledged the closing of the public-domain era. The Federal Land Policy and Management Act of 1976 (FLPMA), codified at 43 U.S.C. § 1701 et seq., declared as national policy that "the public lands be retained in Federal ownership" unless disposal of a particular parcel serves the national interest.

FLPMA effectively ended the general practice of conveying public land intoprivate ownership through homestead-type patents. While certain types of conveyance remain possible under specific statutes, the era of mass land patenting is over.

This legislative shift underscores a basic point: the patent system was a policy tool, and like all policy tools, it operated within the government's discretion — not as a permanent entitlement owed to individuals.

The persistence of alternative interpretations often reflects dissatisfaction with modern systems rather than fidelity to historical ones. It is tempting to believe that an earlier instrument offers escape from contemporary complexity.

That belief, however, assigns to land patents a role they were never designed to play.

Recognizing the original purpose of land patents does not diminish their legitimacy. It restores it.

When understood as tools of transition rather than symbols of exemption, patents make sense within the arc of legal development.

They explain how land entered private ownership.

They do not explain how ownership avoids governance.

This gap between purpose and interpretation is where many well-meaning homeowners become misled.

They assume that older means stronger, or that federal origin implies permanent authority.

In reality, legal strength depends on relevance, enforceability, and alignment with current law.

A document's age does not guarantee its dominance.

Understanding this divergence creates a more grounded perspective.

It allows land patents to be respected without being romanticized, and studied without being weaponized.

That perspective becomes especially important when considering what patents actually grant in practice—and just as importantly, what they do not.

What Land Patents Grant—and What They Do Not Override

At their most basic level, land patents grant private ownership of land that was previously held by a sovereign authority. That grant is real, legally recognized, and historically significant. Without it, private ownership of large portions of the United States would not exist. Acknowledging that significance, however, does not require assigning powers to patents that they do not possess.

What a land patent grants is an initial proprietary interest. It confers legitimacy on the first private owner by documenting that the transfer occurred lawfully.

That legitimacy carries forward through subsequent transfers, forming the foundation of later ownership claims. In that sense, the patent continues to matter as a point of origin. Its role is genealogical rather than operational.

What it does not grant is immunity. It does not override later statutes. It does not negate obligations imposed by law. It does not elevate the holder above regulatory authority. The patent does not exist in competition with the legal system; it exists as part of its history. It is also essential to understand that not all patents conveyed the same bundle of rights. Many patents —particularly those issued under the Stock Raising Homestead Act of 1916 — explicitly reserved mineral rights to the United States. Section 9 of that Act stated that "all entries made and patents issued under the provisions of this Act shall be subject to and contain a reservation to the United States of all the coal and other minerals in the lands so entered and patented." This means that in large portions of the American West, the surface owner who traces title to such a patent does not own the minerals beneath the surface.

The mineral estate was never conveyed. Similarly, patents issued under the Desert Land Act did not include water rights in many jurisdictions that follow the prior appropriation doctrine. The specific language of the authorizing statute and the patent itself must be examined to determine exactly what was transferred. Assuming that a patent conveyed "everything" without reading it is one of the most common and consequential errors in this area. One of the most common misinterpretations involves the idea that patents sit "above" other interests. This idea misunderstands how hierarchy works in property law. Priority is determined by timing, recording, and statutory framework, not by symbolic rank.

A later lien recorded in compliance with law can affect property regardless of how far back the original patent dates. The system does not privilege origin over operation.

Another misunderstanding arises from the assumption that because patents were issued by the federal government, they carry ongoing federal protection. Once land passes into private ownership, the federal role largely recedes.

The land does not remain under federal guardianship. It becomes subject to the same governance as other private property within the state.

Land patents also do not function as defenses against enforcement actions. Courts do not treat them as barriers to foreclosure, taxation, or compliance. When raised as such, they are evaluated for relevance and typically found insufficient to override statutory authority.

In Summa Corp. v. California, 466 U.S. 198 (1984), the Supreme Court confirmed that a federal land patent does not prevent a state from exercising its regulatory authority over the conveyed land.

The patent documents a transfer; it does not dictate the terms of future governance. This outcome is not the result of hostility toward patents; it is the result of applying them within their proper scope.

Understanding what patents do not override is as important as understanding what they grant.

Misplaced reliance on a patent can lead to decisions that increase risk rather than reduce it. Filing documents that assert supremacy without legal basis can invite scrutiny.

Refusing compliance based on misunderstood authority can escalate disputes unnecessarily.

The value of a land patent lies in its clarity, not its confrontation. It clarifies how ownership began. It does not clarify how ownership avoids interaction with law.

When used appropriately, it informs understanding. When used inappropriately, it creates false confidence.

Recognizing these limits does not require abandoning interest in land patents. It requires situating that interest within a realistic framework.

The patent is neither irrelevant nor omnipotent. It is a specific legal instrument with a defined function.

Common Misunderstandings That Create Legal Risk

Misunderstandings about land patents rarely arise from ignorance alone. More often, they emerge from partial knowledge combined with certainty. A homeowner encounters a fragment of information that sounds authoritative, aligns with existing concerns, and promises a clear resolution to complex problems. That fragment then becomes a lens through which everything else is interpreted. Over time, nuance disappears, and what began as curiosity hardens into conviction. It is at this point—not at the moment of discovery—that legal risk begins to accumulate.

One of the most persistent misunderstandings is the belief that a land patent functions as a superior title, capable of overriding all other interests attached to a property. This belief often stems from the word "patent" itself, which suggests exclusivity and finality. In practice, however, property law does not recognize hierarchy in symbolic terms. It recognizes priority, enforceability, and jurisdiction. Treating a patent as a trump card invites actions that are unsupported by the legal system tasked with resolving disputes. When courts are presented with arguments grounded in assumed supremacy rather than applicable law, the outcome is predictable, even if it feels unjust to the person making the claim.

Another dangerous misconception involves the idea that ownership can be perfected retroactively by asserting an original instrument. This line of thinking assumes that if the root of ownership is strong enough, later developments can be disregarded. Yet property law does not operate retroactively in that manner. Later encumbrances, obligations, and restrictions do not disappear because an earlier document is emphasized.

They remain in force because they were created under valid authority and within a functioning legal framework. Ignoring them does not weaken their effect; it merely leaves the property owner unprepared when enforcement occurs. A related misunderstanding concerns the role of recording. Some believe that filing a land patent, or a document referencing it, creates new legal standing simply by entering it into the public record. Recording, however, is not a creative act. It does not generate rights that did not already exist. It provides notice of interests that are legally cognizable.

When a document is recorded without a valid underlying interest, it does not transform into enforceable authority. Instead, it becomes part of the record as a claim, one that may later be challenged or disregarded. In some states, recording documents known to contain false claims can carry criminal penalties. In California, for example, Penal Code § 115 makes it a felony to knowingly procure or offer a false or forged instrument for recording. Similar statutes exist in other jurisdictions. The act of filing is not risk-free.

The risk here is subtle but serious. Recording unsupported assertions can create a false sense of security. A homeowner may believe that action has been taken, protection has been established, and risk has been reduced. In reality, nothing substantive has changed. Worse, the act of recording may draw attention to misunderstandings that otherwise would have remained dormant. Legal systems are not obligated to correct misconceptions proactively, but they respond decisively when disputes arise.

Another common error is assuming that the federal origin of a land patent places property beyond state authority. This misunderstanding often arises from conflating federal conveyance with federal jurisdiction. While the federal government originally transferred the land, it does not retain ongoing governance over privately owned parcels.

Property regulation, taxation, and enforcement are administered primarily at the state and local levels. Invoking federal origin as a shield against those authorities misunderstands how sovereignty is distributed in practice.

This misconception is particularly risky because it encourages confrontational behavior. Homeowners may refuse compliance, delay obligations, or challenge authority based on an assumption that jurisdiction has been misapplied. When those challenges fail—as they often do—the resulting consequences are rarely minor. Penalties accrue, enforcement escalates, and options narrow. What began as an attempt to assert control ends in diminished flexibility. Courts have addressed this pattern directly.

In United States v. Benabe, 654 F.3d 753 (7th Cir. 2011), the Seventh Circuit stated: "Regardless of an individual's claimed status of descent, be it as a 'sovereign citizen,' a 'secured-party creditor,' or a 'flesh-and-blood human being,' that person is not beyond the jurisdiction of the courts. These theories should be rejected summarily, however they are presented." Land patent arguments are frequently raised alongside these theories and receive the same treatment.

Equally problematic is the belief that courts are either unaware of land patents or deliberately ignore them. This narrative portrays the legal system as either incompetent or hostile, positioning the homeowner as a lone holder of suppressed truth. While emotionally compelling, this belief discourages realistic assessment. Courts are not unfamiliar with land patents. They are familiar with them precisely because they appear regularly in filings, often raised in contexts where they do not apply. The consistent judicial response is not evidence of ignorance; it is evidence of interpretation grounded in law.

Another misunderstanding involves the expectation that land patents provide protection against taxation. This idea often circulates alongside broader arguments about sovereignty and property rights. In reality, taxation attaches to property based on jurisdiction and statute, not on the historical form of conveyance.
A patent does not exempt property from tax assessment any more than a deed does.
Acting on the assumption that it does can lead to compounding penalties and loss of standing long before the issue reaches a courtroom.

Perhaps the most damaging misunderstanding is the belief that certainty itself is protective. Confidence, when unsupported by accurate understanding, can be dangerous. It encourages homeowners to act decisively when caution would be wiser. It discourages verification. It replaces inquiry with assertion. Legal systems do not reward confidence; they reward alignment with recognized authority and procedure.

What makes these misunderstandings especially risky is that they often circulate in communities where skepticism of institutions is normalized. Questioning authority is not inherently problematic. Blind rejection of it, however, leaves individuals exposed. Property law is not negotiated through belief. It is enforced through processes that do not adapt to personal interpretations.

Risk also increases when homeowners assume that professional advice is unnecessary because the truth has already been discovered. This assumption isolates individuals from corrective input. It frames disagreement as hostility rather than expertise. When professional guidance is dismissed in favor of self-reinforcing narratives, mistakes compound quietly until they become unavoidable. None of these misunderstandings arise from malice.

They arise from an information environment that rewards simplicity and certainty over accuracy and restraint. The antidote is not fear, but discipline. Discipline in how claims are evaluated. Discipline in distinguishing documentation from authority. Discipline in recognizing the limits of any single instrument, no matter how compelling its language may be.

Chapter 3 – How Land Patents Interact With Modern Property Law

Federal Origins vs State-Based Property Systems

The confusion surrounding land patents often begins with a single, deceptively simple assumption: because land patents originate from federal authority, they must continue to operate primarily within a federal legal sphere. This assumption feels intuitive. After all, the federal government issued the patent. It conveyed the land. It signed the document. For many readers, that origin suggests an ongoing federal relationship, one that overrides or eclipses state-level authority. The reality is more nuanced, and far less dramatic.

When the federal government conveyed land through a patent, it was exercising a specific power at a specific moment: the power to dispose of public land. That power derives from the Property Clause of the Constitution, Article IV, Section 3, Clause 2, which grants Congress authority "to dispose of and make all needful Rules and Regulations respecting the Territory or other Property belonging to the United States." That power was transactional, not supervisory. Once the conveyance occurred, the federal government's role changed fundamentally. The land exited the federal inventory and entered the legal universe of private property. From that point forward, governance did not remain federal by default. It shifted to the same systems that regulate all privately owned land within the state where the property is located.

This shift is not a loophole or a historical accident. It reflects the constitutional structure of the United States. While the federal government has enumerated powers, property law—particularly the regulation of privately held land—has traditionally been administered at the state level. States define property interests, establish recording systems, enforce land-use regulations, and adjudicate disputes. Counties and municipalities, in turn, carry out many of these functions on the ground.

Understanding this division of authority is essential. Federal origin does not imply federal immunity. A land patent marks the end of federal ownership, not the beginning of federal oversight. Once land becomes private, it is subject to the same legal environment as other private property within the state. Taxes are assessed under state law. Transfers are governed by state statutes. Disputes are resolved in state courts unless a distinct federal issue is present. This allocation of authority is reinforced by the Tenth Amendment, which reserves to the states all powers not delegated to the federal government. The regulation of private property within state borders is among the most traditional of those reserved powers.

The persistence of federal symbolism in land patent discussions often obscures this reality. The presence of federal seals, historical language, and references to sovereignty can create the impression that the patent exists outside ordinary legal channels. In truth, the patent's authority was fully exercised when the land was conveyed. After that point, its role became historical rather than operational.
State-based property systems are not secondary or derivative. They are comprehensive legal frameworks developed over centuries to manage ownership, use, and transfer of land. These systems do not compete with federal patents; they absorb them. The patent becomes part of the property's legal ancestry, not its governing charter.

This distinction also explains why invoking federal origin rarely alters outcomes in modern disputes. Courts do not ignore federal documents, but they do not treat them as jurisdictional trump cards. The principle was settled nearly two centuries ago in Wilcox v. Jackson, 38 U.S. 498 (1839), when the Supreme Court held that the question of whether title has passed is governed by federal law, but once it has passed, the property is "subject to state legislation, so far as that legislation is consistent with the admission that the title passed and vested according to the laws of the United States." The question is not where the land came from, but how it is regulated now. The legal system is oriented toward present authority, not historical ceremony.

For homeowners, this division of power can feel counterintuitive. It is natural to assume that the entity that granted the land retains some special relationship to it. In practice, however, that relationship ends with the grant itself. The stability of private ownership depends on the predictability of state governance, not on lingering federal involvement.

Recognizing this structure does not diminish the significance of land patents. It clarifies their place. They explain how land entered private ownership, but they do not define how that ownership functions today. That function is shaped by the laws of the state and enforced through local institutions. Understanding that shift—from federal transaction to state governance—removes much of the mystery surrounding how land patents interact with modern property law.

Once that framework is clear, attention naturally turns to the mechanisms through which state authority is exercised and documented. These mechanisms are not abstract. They operate through records, offices, and courts that translate legal theory into practical outcomes.

Recording Statutes, County Authority, and Court

Modern property law does not operate through declarations of belief or appeals to history. t operates through systems designed to provide notice, establish priority, and resolve conflict. At the center of those systems are recording statutes, county recording offices, and courts. Together, they form the infrastructure that allows ownership to be recognized and enforced in real-world situations.

Recording statutes exist for a simple but critical reason: property interests must be visible to be reliable. When interests are recorded, they become part of a public ledger that anyone can consult. This transparency reduces disputes, protects purchasers, and allows courts to determine priority when claims conflict. Without recording systems, property ownership would rely on private knowledge and personal authority, conditions that historically led to instability and violence. Not all recording statutes work the same way.

American states follow one of three models, and the differences carry real consequences when competing interests collide.

Under a race statute, the first party to record prevails, regardless of whether they knew about a prior unrecorded interest; only North Carolina and Louisiana (in part) still follow this approach. Under a notice statute, a subsequent purchaser who acquires an interest in good faith and without notice of a prior unrecorded claim prevails, even if they have not yet recorded; states following this model include Alabama, Arizona, Connecticut, Florida, Illinois, Kansas, Massachusetts, Missouri, Oklahoma, and Texas, among others. Under a race-notice statute — the most common type, used by roughly thirty states including California, New York, Colorado, Pennsylvania, and Washington — a subsequent purchaser must both lack notice of the prior claim and record first.

These distinctions apply to every type of recorded interest, including deeds, mortgages, liens, and any document referencing a land patent. Understanding which system governs in a given state is not optional; it determines who wins when claims overlap. County recording offices serve as the custodians of this system. They do not judge the validity of every document presented to them, nor do they certify legal conclusions. Their role is administrative. They receive documents, index them, and make them publicly accessible. The power of a recorded document does not come from the act of recording itself, but from the legal validity of the interest it represents.

This distinction is frequently misunderstood. Recording a document does not transform it into an enforceable right. It merely gives notice of a claimed interest. Courts determine whether that interest is legally cognizable. When a document asserts authority that the law does not recognize, recording it does not cure that defect. It simply makes the claim visible.

Courts, therefore, play a central role in translating recorded interests into enforceable outcomes. They interpret statutes, evaluate evidence, and apply precedent. When disputes arise, courts look to the public record to understand the history of a property. They assess whether interests were created lawfully, whether they were recorded properly, and how they interact with one another.

Land patents enter this process as historical records. They are part of the property's documented past, but they do not occupy a privileged position in the adjudicative process.

Courts do not elevate them above later instruments simply because of their age or origin. Instead, they consider them in context, alongside all other recorded interests.

When genuine disputes exist about who owns a property or whether a particular interest is valid, the standard remedy is a quiet title action — a lawsuit filed to establish ownership and remove "clouds" on the title.

The federal Quiet Title Act, 28 U.S.C. § 2409a, even allows private parties to name the United States as a defendant in title disputes involving federal interests. Each state has its own quiet title procedures as well — for example, 12 O.S. § 1141 in Oklahoma or F.S. Chapter 65 in Florida. These are the tools the legal system provides for resolving ownership questions.

Filing unsupported documents referencing a patent is not one of them.County authority extends beyond recordkeeping. Local governments enforce zoning, building codes, and land-use regulations. These authorities are grounded in state law and applied uniformly to properties within their jurisdiction. A land patent does not exempt property from these requirements. Compliance is determined by current law, not by historical conveyance.

The interaction between recording offices and courts underscores an important principle: property law is procedural as much as it is substantive. Rights exist because they are recognized through established processes. Skipping or misunderstanding those processes does not preserve rights; it undermines them.

Homeowners sometimes encounter frustration when recording offices refuse to assign special status to documents referencing land patents. That frustration often stems from the expectation that historical authority should translate into administrative deference. In reality, recording offices are not empowered to make legal judgments. They operate within narrowly defined roles. Expecting them to validate legal theories exceeds their function.

Courts, by contrast, do make judgments, but they do so within a framework that prioritizes coherence and predictability. They are tasked with maintaining the integrity of the property system as a whole. Arguments that disrupt that coherence without legal foundation are unlikely to succeed, regardless of how compelling they may sound.

Understanding how recording statutes, county authority, and courts interact reveals why property law resists shortcuts. The system is designed to be slow, deliberate, and resistant to unilateral claims. That resistance is not hostility; it is stability. It ensures that ownership remains reliable across generations.

This procedural reality leads directly to one of the most common points of confusion: the assumption that land patents, by virtue of their origin, automatically override local law. That assumption does not survive contact with the mechanisms described above.

Why Land Patents Do Not Automatically Supersede Local Law

The belief that land patents override local law often arises from a misunderstanding of hierarchy. It assumes that because the patent came first, and because it was issued by a sovereign authority, it must outrank all subsequent legal structures.

This assumption treats law as a vertical ladder rather than a coordinated system. In practice, property law functions horizontally, with authority distributed according to jurisdiction and subject matter. Local law governs because it is empowered to do so. Zoning ordinances, tax codes, and land-use regulations are enacted under state authority.

They apply to all property within their scope, regardless of how that property entered private ownership. A land patent does not remove land from that scope. It does not place property in a legal enclave. It integrates it into a regulatory environment. Supremacy is often misunderstood in this context. The Supremacy Clause of the Constitution, Article VI, Clause 2, provides that federal law is "the supreme Law of the Land" when it conflicts with state law. But a conflict must actually exist. Federal preemption requires either an express congressional directive, a federal regulatory scheme so pervasive that it occupies the field, or a direct impossibility of complying with both federal and state law simultaneously Land patents do not create an ongoing federal regulatory domain.

They document a completed conveyance. There is no conflict between a patent and local law because they do not govern the same thing. One records how ownership began; the other governs how ownership operates.

Courts consistently recognize this distinction. When land patents are raised as defenses against local enforcement, they are evaluated for relevance. The typical judicial response is not dismissal of the patent itself, but clarification of its limited function.
The patent is acknowledged as part of the historical record, then set aside as inapplicable to the issue at hand. The constitutionality of local zoning was settled nearly a century ago in Village of Euclid v. Ambler Realty Co., 272 U.S. 365 (1926), where the Supreme Court upheld municipal zoning as a valid exercise of state police power. That holding has never been overturned. A land patent, regardless of its vintage, does not furnish grounds to relitigate it.

This outcome surprises many homeowners because it conflicts with narratives that frame local law as subordinate or illegitimate. Those narratives often rely on abstract interpretations of sovereignty rather than on how legal authority is actually exercised. Property law does not operate on philosophical hierarchy; it operates on jurisdictional competence.

Another source of confusion lies in the language of exemption. Some believe that because a land patent represents private ownership, it exempts property from public obligations. In reality, private ownership is the condition that triggers many obligations. Taxes are assessed precisely because property is privately held. Regulations apply because land use affects the community.
Exemption would undermine the very stability that makes ownership valuable.
Local law does not erase ownership. It shapes it. That shaping is not arbitrary; it is the result of legislative processes, public accountability, and judicial review. A land patent does not stand outside those processes. It stands at the beginning of a chain that leads directly into them.

Understanding why patents do not supersede local law also helps explain why attempts to assert them as overrides often escalate conflict. Local authorities are not equipped to reinterpret historical conveyances. They are tasked with enforcing current law. When confronted with arguments that challenge their jurisdiction, they respond through enforcement mechanisms, not philosophical debate.

This dynamic creates a cycle of frustration for homeowners who expect recognition where none is forthcoming. The expectation itself is the problem. It is based on a model of authority that does not exist in modern property law. Adjusting that model reduces risk and restores alignment with reality.

Recognizing the limits of land patents in relation to local law is not an act of surrender. It is an act of precision. It allows homeowners to focus on strategies that operate within the system rather than against it. Precision, in property matters, is a form of protection.

How Courts Typically View Patent-Based Arguments Today

When land patents appear in modern courtrooms, they do not arrive as unfamiliar artifacts from a forgotten legal era. Judges, clerks, and opposing counsel have seen them before, often many times. They appear in filings attached to motions, cited in affidavits, referenced in pro se arguments, or raised defensively when enforcement actions loom.

What distinguishes these appearances is not novelty, but context. Courts do not ask whether land patents exist. They ask whether the way they are being invoked has legal relevance to the dispute at hand. Courts are pragmatic institutions. Their task is not to resolve philosophical questions about sovereignty or historical purity, but to apply current law to concrete facts. When a patent-based argument is presented, the court's attention turns immediately to function. What is this document being offered to prove?
What legal effect is being claimed? Does that effect align with existing statutes, precedent, and jurisdictional authority? These questions shape the court's response far more than the age or language of the document itself.

In most cases, land patents are treated as evidence of origin rather than as sources of ongoing authority. Courts acknowledge that a patent demonstrates lawful conveyance from the government to a private party. That acknowledgment, however, is usually where the inquiry ends. The patent's relevance is confined to establishing that the land was properly privatized at a certain point in history. It does not extend to altering present-day obligations, extinguishing recorded interests, or negating regulatory authority.

Judicial opinions consistently reflect this approach. When patents are raised in disputes involving taxation, foreclosure, zoning, or enforcement, courts analyze whether the patent has any bearing on the specific legal issue. Almost invariably, they conclude that it does not. This conclusion is not framed as hostility toward patents, but as recognition of their limited scope.

Courts are explicit in stating that historical conveyance does not confer exemption from laws enacted long after that conveyance occurred. There are narrow exceptions.

In Michigan, for instance, courts have recognized that a land patent can be relevant in establishing ownership of submerged lands — situations where the original patent description included areas that later became lake bottom.

But even in those cases, the patent serves as evidence of the original conveyance boundaries, not as a source of immunity from regulation. The exception proves the rule: patents matter when the question is what was originally conveyed, not when the question is what law now applies.

Patent-based arguments often falter because they attempt to import abstract principles into procedural settings. Courts are procedural by design. They rely on statutes that define rights and remedies. They require claims to be grounded in applicable law.

Arguments that rely on broad assertions of sovereignty or supremacy without tying those assertions to current legal authority are viewed as conclusory.

They lack the specificity courts require to grant relief. Another factor shaping judicial response is consistency. Courts are acutely aware of the need for predictable outcomes.

Property law depends on predictability more than almost any other area of law. Allowing historical documents to override modern frameworks would destabilize ownership across entire jurisdictions.

Judges are not inclined to open that door, particularly when existing law provides clear guidance. This does not mean courts refuse to engage with patent-related claims. They engage with them carefully, often explaining why the argument fails rather than dismissing it outright.
Opinions frequently clarify that while patents are valid historical instruments, they do not alter the distribution of authority between federal, state, and local governments. They do not invalidate statutes. They do not displace recorded interests created under later law.

Courts also consider intent. When patent-based arguments are raised defensively, courts examine whether they are being used to avoid compliance rather than to clarify rights.
Attempts to use patents as shields against obligations are viewed skeptically, particularly when those obligations arise from statutes of general applicability. Judges are trained to distinguish between legitimate claims of right and efforts to sidestep enforcement.

Another recurring theme in judicial treatment is the emphasis on jurisdiction. Courts operate within defined boundaries. They cannot enforce authority that does not exist, nor can they ignore authority that does. Patent-based arguments that challenge jurisdiction without legal foundation are often rejected swiftly, not because the court is unwilling to listen, but because jurisdiction is not negotiable. It is established by law, not by interpretation. When patents are raised in appellate contexts, the analysis becomes even more explicit.

Appellate courts often take the opportunity to clarify misconceptions, not only for the parties involved but for the broader legal community. These opinions tend to emphasize that property rights are defined by current law and that historical instruments do not create parallel systems of governance. The tone is corrective rather than dismissive, reflecting the courts' awareness that confusion persists. One of the most comprehensive judicial examinations of pseudolegal property theories came in Meads v. Meads, 2012 ABQB 571, a Canadian decision by Associate Chief Justice Rooke of the Alberta Court of Queen's Bench.

Though a Canadian case, it is frequently cited in American legal scholarship for its exhaustive taxonomy of pseudolegal arguments — including land patent claims, sovereign citizen theories, and "strawman" doctrines — and its systematic explanation of why each fails.

American courts confronting similar arguments have drawn on the same analytical framework. One of the most important aspects of judicial treatment is what courts do not do. They do not debate ideology. They do not engage with narratives about hidden authority or suppressed truth.

They do not weigh the moral appeal of absolute ownership. Their focus remains narrow: what does the law recognize, and how does it apply here? Anything outside that focus is treated as extraneous.

For homeowners, understanding this judicial posture is critical. It reveals that success in property disputes does not come from invoking powerful-sounding documents, but from aligning arguments with recognized authority.

Courts reward coherence, not conviction. They respond to law, not belief. This reality also explains why reliance on patent-based arguments often increases legal exposure.

When courts repeatedly reject such arguments, patterns emerge. Litigants may be labeled as frivolous. Filings may be scrutinized more closely.

Credibility can erode. In some jurisdictions, courts may impose sanctions under rules such as Federal Rule of Civil Procedure 11, which authorizes penalties for filings that are not "warranted by existing law or by a nonfrivolous argument for extending, modifying, or reversing existing law." None of these outcomes serve the homeowner's interests.

This reality also explains why reliance on patent-based arguments often increases legal exposure. When courts repeatedly reject such arguments, patterns emerge. Litigants may be labeled as frivolous. Filings may be scrutinized more closely. Credibility can erode. None of these outcomes serve the homeowner's interests.

Chapter 4 – Tracing the Origin of a Property Without Getting Lost

Understanding Land Origin Without Becoming a Historian

For many homeowners, the idea of tracing the origin of their property carries an intimidating weight. It conjures images of dusty archives, indecipherable maps, and centuries-old documents written in language that feels deliberately opaque.
That impression alone is enough to discourage inquiry, or worse, to push people toward oversimplified explanations that promise certainty without effort. The truth lies somewhere between those extremes. Understanding where a property originated does not require becoming a historian, but it does require understanding what questions actually matter.

Land origin refers to the point at which a parcel first entered private ownership under recognized authority. That moment is foundational, but it is not all-encompassing. Knowing how land originated helps establish legitimacy, but it does not explain everything that followed. Problems arise when origin is treated as destiny, as if the circumstances of first conveyance dictate all subsequent legal realities. They do not. Origin explains how private ownership began, not how it must operate indefinitely.

The most common mistake people make when exploring land origin is assuming that deeper automatically means stronger. They believe that the further back they go, the more authoritative their findings become. In practice, relevance diminishes with distance unless the information discovered has a direct bearing on present conditions.
Property law values continuity, not antiquity. An uninterrupted, well-documented chain matters far more than a dramatic point of origin disconnected from current records.
Another source of confusion is the tendency to conflate historical curiosity with legal necessity. It is entirely reasonable to want to know how land was first conveyed, who received it, and under what authority. That knowledge can be informative and even satisfying. It becomes problematic only when it is treated as a substitute for understanding the current legal environment. Land origin is a starting line, not a destination.

Understanding origin without getting lost requires a shift in mindset. Rather than asking, "How far back can I go?" a more useful question is, "What does knowing this change?" If the answer is unclear, the research may be drifting from relevance into obsession.

Legal systems are built to function without requiring owners to reconstruct centuries of history. That design is intentional. Stability depends on accessible records and defined points of reliance.

Historical land systems were often complex precisely because there was no centralized, standardized method of documentation. Over time, property law evolved to reduce that complexity. Recording systems were developed to limit how far back one needed to look to establish ownership.

Statutes of limitation, marketable title acts, and recording priorities exist to prevent endless excavation of the past. Marketable title acts are particularly relevant here.

At least seventeen states — including Connecticut, Florida, Illinois, Indiana, Iowa, Kansas, Michigan, Minnesota, Nebraska, North Carolina, North Dakota, Ohio, Oklahoma, South Dakota, Utah, Vermont, and Wyoming — have enacted statutes that set a defined lookback period, typically thirty to forty years, beyond which most prior claims and interests are extinguished unless affirmatively preserved by recording.

Florida's Marketable Record Title Act (F.S.Ch. 712), for example, establishes a thirty-year root-of-title rule. In practice, this means that in states with such acts, the original land patent is almost never examined in a routine title search. The search begins at the statutory root of title, not at the dawn of ownership. Ignoring these mechanisms in favor of raw historical inquiry undermines the very protections they provide.

Another trap lies in interpreting historical language through modern assumptions.

Terms used in early conveyances often carried meanings specific to their time and place. Reading them as literal, timeless commands can lead to misunderstandings. Legal language evolves, and interpretation follows suit.

Courts do not read historical documents in isolation; they interpret them through established principles that account for context, intent, and subsequent development.

This does not mean historical research has no value. It means its value lies in clarification rather than control. Knowing whether land originated from federal disposition, state grant, or colonial charter can help frame later developments. It can explain why certain records exist or why others do not. What it cannot do is override the legal structures that now govern the property.

Approaching land origin responsibly involves setting boundaries. Curiosity is directed, not limitless. Questions are framed with purpose. Research stops when additional information no longer changes understanding. This discipline protects homeowners from becoming trapped in narratives that privilege discovery over coherence.

The goal is orientation, not excavation. Orientation means knowing where the property came from well enough to understand how it entered the legal system, without mistaking that entry point for a source of ongoing authority. When that balance is achieved, land origin becomes a useful reference rather than a source of confusion. That orientation naturally leads to another distinction that often surprises property owners: not all states share the same foundational relationship to public land.

Understanding that difference adds clarity, but only if it is approached with the same restraint.

Public-Domain States vs State-Land States

One of the least understood aspects of land origin in the United States is that not all land entered private ownership through the same pathway. The country's expansion unfolded unevenly, shaped by treaties, territorial governance, and evolving federal policy.
As a result, states fall into two broad categories based on how land was originally held and distributed: public-domain states and state-land states. This distinction is real, but it is often exaggerated beyond its practical significance.

Public-domain states are those in which the federal government held large tracts of land before transferring them into private ownership. Most western and midwestern states fall into this category.
The thirty public-domain states are: Alabama, Alaska, Arizona, Arkansas, California, Colorado, Florida, Idaho, Illinois, Indiana, Iowa, Kansas, Louisiana, Michigan, Minnesota, Mississippi, Missouri, Montana, Nebraska, Nevada, New Mexico, North Dakota, Ohio, Oklahoma, Oregon, South Dakota, Utah, Washington, Wisconsin, and Wyoming.
In these states, land typically entered private hands through federal conveyance, often following survey and compliance with statutory requirements. State-land states, by contrast, include areas where land was originally controlled by colonies, states, or sovereign entities other than the federal government.

These twenty states and their territories are: the original thirteen colonies, Connecticut, Delaware, Georgia, Maryland, Massachusetts, New Hampshire, New Jersey, New York, North Carolina, Pennsylvania, Rhode Island, South Carolina, and Virginia — plus Vermont, Kentucky, Tennessee, Maine, West Virginia, Texas, and Hawaii.
Each of these states developed its own system of initial land conveyance.
In the original colonies, grants came from colonial governors or proprietors under Crown authority.
In Texas, the General Land Office (glo.texas.gov) manages records of grants issued under Spanish, Mexican, and Republic of Texas authority. In Hawaii, the unique Mahele of 1848 divided lands between the king, chiefs, and government, with subsequent patents issued under Hawaiian and later American authority.

In these jurisdictions, private ownership developed through different mechanisms.
This distinction matters for historical understanding, but it does not create parallel legal universes. Regardless of how land originated, once it enters private ownership, it becomes subject to the same state-based property system that governs all privately held land within that state's borders. The pathway in does not determine the rules that apply afterward.

Confusion often arises when people assume that public-domain origin grants land a special status. Because federal involvement feels significant, it is tempting to treat public-domain land as fundamentally different from land that originated under state authority. In practice, the difference is administrative, not functional. The legal system does not maintain separate regimes based on origin. It integrates all private land into a unified framework.

Another misunderstanding stems from assuming that state-land states lack any equivalent to land patents. While the instruments differ, the function is similar. Every system requires a method for establishing original private ownership. The form that method takes varies, but its role is consistent. Focusing too narrowly on one type of document risks missing the broader pattern.
The public-domain versus state-land distinction is often used rhetorically to imply hierarchy. Public-domain land is framed as purer, more legitimate, or more authoritative. This framing has no basis in modern law. Courts do not assign greater weight to ownership based on origin. They assess rights based on present recognition and compliance.

Understanding this distinction responsibly involves resisting the urge to read significance where none exists. It is a descriptive category, not a normative one. It explains history; it does not confer advantage. When homeowners grasp this, they are less likely to be misled by claims that promise special treatment based on origin alone.
This distinction also helps clarify why searching for federal records may be irrelevant in certain states. In state-land jurisdictions, federal databases will not contain origin information because the federal government was never the source of conveyance.

A homeowner in Pennsylvania searching the BLM-GLO Records database for a federal land patent will find nothing — not because the records are missing, but because Pennsylvania's land was conveyed through William Penn's proprietary grants, and its patents are held at the Pennsylvania State Archives (phmc.state.pa.us), not at the BLM.

Similarly, Texas land records are maintained by the Texas General Land Office, and Connecticut's colonial-era records reside at the Connecticut State Library.Expecting those records to exist leads to frustration and misinterpretation.

Recognizing which category a state falls into can prevent wasted effort and misplaced expectations. It helps align research with reality rather than forcing reality to fit a preconceived narrative. That alignment is critical for maintaining clarity as inquiry moves from theory to documentation.

Once that alignment is established, attention naturally turns to the practical question of where information is actually stored and how it should be handled. Official databases can be valuable tools, but only when they are approached with appropriate caution.

Using Official Databases Responsibly (BLM, State Archives)

Official databases occupy a peculiar position in discussions about land origin. On one hand, they are treated as definitive sources, capable of resolving all uncertainty. On the other, they are dismissed as incomplete or manipulated when their contents fail to support certain claims. Neither view is accurate.

These databases are tools — powerful ones — but they have limits that must be respected. Federal databases maintained by agencies such as the Bureau of Land Management exist to preserve records related to public land disposition.

They document surveys, patents, and related administrative actions. The primary federal resource is the BLM General Land Office Records website at glorecords.blm.gov.

It provides free online access to images of more than five million federal land title records issued between 1820 and the present, including patent documents, survey plats, master title plats, and field notes. To search, a user can enter a patentee's name, or navigate by state, land office, township, range, and section number.

Each patent record typically shows the patentee's name, the date of issuance, the legal description of the land, the type of entry (homestead, cash sale, military warrant, etc.), and the authorizing statute. The site also provides images of the original patent documents, many of which bear the signature of the sitting President.

However, the BLM-GLO database only covers the thirty public-domain states. It does not contain records for the original thirteen states, Texas, Hawaii, or other state-land states. When used correctly, these records can confirm whether land was conveyed by federal authority and provide insight into the circumstances of that conveyance. What they cannot do is explain how ownership functions today or resolve disputes that arise long after conveyance occurred. State archives serve a different but complementary role. They preserve records generated under state authority, including grants, early transfers, and legislative actions. For state-land states, these archives are the primary source of origin records. The Pennsylvania State Archives (phmc.state.pa.us) holds patent index images from 1684 to 1957.

The Texas General Land Office (glo.texas.gov) maintains a searchable Land Grant Database covering Spanish, Mexican, and Republic of Texas grants. The National Archives in Washington, D.C., holds the land entry case files (Record Group 49) for the public-domain states, which contain the application papers behind each patent — often including genealogical information, affidavits, and proof-of-compliance documents not visible in the patent itself.
These case files can be requested through the National Archives website at archives.gov/research/land. Like federal databases, state archives are repositories of information, not arbiters of meaning.

Their value lies in accuracy and preservation, not interpretation. The most common mistake made when consulting official databases is assuming that presence equals power. Finding a record can feel decisive, as if discovery itself settles the matter.
In reality, a record confirms that something happened; it does not determine how that event should be understood in isolation. Interpretation requires context, and context often lies outside the database itself.

Another pitfall is overreliance on partial records. Not all documents are digitized. Not all records survived intact. Gaps are common, especially in older materials. Treating absence as evidence of suppression or invalidity is a leap that introduces error.
Silence in the record often reflects administrative reality, not legal significance. Responsible use of databases involves approaching them with specific questions rather than vague expectations. Searching with a clear purpose reduces the temptation to draw conclusions from unrelated findings. It also helps distinguish between relevant and incidental information. Context matters as much as content. A patent record may confirm origin, but it does not negate later transfers. A survey map may illustrate boundaries, but it does not resolve disputes. Databases provide pieces, not pictures. Assembling those pieces into a coherent understanding requires restraint.

Another risk arises when database findings are treated as self-authenticating. While official records carry presumptive reliability, their legal effect depends on how they are used. Courts rely on records as evidence, not as arguments. A document does not speak for itself; it must be situated within applicable law.

Responsible engagement with databases also means recognizing when research has reached its limit. Continuing to search after relevant information has been found often leads to confirmation bias. New findings are interpreted to reinforce existing beliefs rather than to test them. At that point, research becomes advocacy, and clarity suffers.

Used wisely, official databases can ground understanding. Used carelessly, they can fuel misinterpretation. The difference lies not in access, but in discipline.

How to Verify Information Without Jumping to Conclusions

Tracing land origin inevitably produces moments of apparent discovery. A name appears in an old record. A date aligns with a known historical period. A document carries official formatting and authoritative language.

At those moments, the temptation to conclude—to declare meaning, power, or consequence—is strong.

Verification, however, is not about confirmation. It is about calibration.

The difference between the two determines whether research clarifies understanding or quietly distorts it.

Verification begins with recognizing that information does not speak on its own.

Documents are inert. They acquire meaning only when interpreted within a framework that accounts for authority, timing, and applicability. A record can be authentic and still irrelevant. It can be accurate and still incomplete. Jumping to conclusions often happens when authenticity is mistaken for applicability.

One of the most common verification errors occurs when a document is treated as self-executing.

A land record, for example, may accurately show that a conveyance occurred under federal authority. That fact alone does not establish how the land is governed today, how it is taxed, or how disputes are resolved. Verification requires separating what a document proves from what it merely suggests. The former is narrow; the latter is often speculative.

Context is the first stabilizing force. Every document exists within a legal and administrative environment. Knowing who issued it, under what authority, and for what purpose matters more than its wording. A patent issued to transfer land does not carry the same implications as a statute enacted to regulate land use. Treating them as interchangeable sources of authority collapses distinct functions into a single narrative, which is precisely how misunderstandings gain momentum.

Another critical aspect of verification is chronology. Property law is sequential. Later actions do not erase earlier ones, but they often qualify them. When evaluating information, the question is not simply whether something occurred, but what happened afterward. Verification that ignores sequence risks assigning controlling significance to events that have long since been integrated into a broader legal structure.

This is where many well-intentioned researchers falter. They discover an early record and assume it operates independently of everything that followed. In reality, property systems are cumulative. Each transfer, encumbrance, and regulation builds upon the last. Verification requires tracing continuity, not isolating origin.

Language itself can be deceptive. Older documents often use terminology that feels absolute to modern readers. Words like "forever," "absolute," or "exclusive" appear frequently in historical conveyances.

Verification requires understanding how such language was conventionally used at the time. Legal drafting has always employed emphatic phrasing. That emphasis does not override subsequent law, nor does it imply immunity from governance. Treating rhetorical strength as legal force is a common analytical error.

Another safeguard against premature conclusions is triangulation. No single document should be relied upon in isolation. Verifying information means checking whether multiple sources align in substance, not just in appearance. If a claim rests on one document interpreted in one way, it deserves scrutiny. If it is supported by consistent treatment across statutes, records, and judicial interpretation, it carries more weight. Consistency across independent systems is a far stronger indicator of reliability than dramatic language in a single source.

Verification also involves understanding institutional roles. Recording offices preserve documents. They do not validate legal theories. Archives store records. They do not confer authority. Courts interpret law. They do not rewrite history. Confusing these roles leads to misplaced confidence. A document preserved in an archive is not endorsed by the archive.

A filing accepted for recording is not approved by the recorder.
Verification requires respecting these boundaries. A practical approach to verification might follow these steps.
First, identify what the document actually says — not what it seems to promise, but what it records as a factual matter.
Second, determine the authority under which it was issued: which statute, which office, which level of government.
Third, trace what happened after the document was created: were there subsequent transfers, encumbrances, or regulations that modified the interests it describes?
Fourth, check whether the document's claims are consistent with how courts and recording offices in the relevant jurisdiction actually treat such instruments today.
Fifth, consult a licensed attorney or title professional before taking any action based on historical findings. This sequence is not glamorous, but it is protective. It separates genuine insight from wishful interpretation.
Equally important is resisting narrative completion. Humans are wired to seek coherent stories. When fragments of information appear to fit together, the impulse is to connect them into a larger meaning. In property research, this impulse can be dangerous.
Gaps in records are often administrative, not conspiratorial. Silence does not imply suppression. Absence does not imply invalidity. Verification requires tolerating uncertainty rather than filling it with assumption.

Another risk factor is emotional investment. When research is motivated by fear, frustration, or a desire for control, conclusions tend to form quickly. Verification slows that process deliberately. It introduces friction. It forces questions like, "What would contradict this?" and "What authority actually enforces this?" Those questions are uncomfortable precisely because they test belief rather than reinforce it.

Responsible verification also means knowing when to stop. There is a point at which additional information no longer increases clarity. Continuing beyond that point often leads to selective interpretation, where new findings are forced to support an existing conclusion.
At that stage, research becomes advocacy, and understanding suffers.

Verification is not skepticism for its own sake. It is discipline applied to curiosity. It does not dismiss discovery; it contextualizes it. It does not deny complexity; it manages it. The goal is not certainty, but proportion—knowing how much weight a piece of information can reasonably bear.

For homeowners, this approach offers a form of protection that no document can provide. It prevents overconfidence.
It reduces exposure to misleading claims. It replaces reaction with reflection. When verification is practiced consistently, conclusions emerge more slowly, but they rest on firmer ground.

Chapter 5 – The Chain of Title: Where Real Strength or Weakness Exists

Why Chain of Title Matters More Than Ideology

Property ownership does not fail or succeed on the strength of ideas. It stands or collapses on documentation. This reality is uncomfortable for anyone drawn to grand explanations about sovereignty, original authority, or hidden mechanisms of control, because documentation lacks drama. It is procedural, incremental, and often tedious. Yet it is precisely this unglamorous quality that gives it power. In the legal world, strength is measured not by conviction but by continuity.

The chain of title is the documented history of how ownership interests in a property have passed from one party to another over time. It is not a philosophical construct. It is a practical one.

Courts, lenders, insurers, and regulators rely on it because it answers a basic question with verifiable evidence: how did this property come to be owned in its present form, and were those transitions legally valid?

Ideology offers narratives.

The chain of title offers proof. When disputes arise, proof prevails.

Many homeowners encounter the concept of chain of title only indirectly, often during a purchase, refinancing, or legal review. A title search is ordered. A report is generated. Problems, if any, are flagged.

Once the transaction closes, the chain fades into the background again. A title search is typically conducted by a title company or abstractor who examines the public records at the county recorder's office, tracing each transfer, mortgage, lien, easement, and other recorded interest affecting the property. In states with marketable title acts, the search may begin at the statutory root of title — often thirty to forty years back — rather than at the original patent. In states without such acts, the search may need to extend further.

The resulting title report or abstract identifies the current state of the title, including any defects, encumbrances, or unresolved claims. Title insurance is then issued based on the findings of that search, with specific exceptions listed for known issues.

This distance allows misconceptions to grow. People begin to assume that ownership is either settled forever or fundamentally insecure, depending on which narrative they encounter.

The truth is more precise. Ownership is secure when the chain is coherent. It is vulnerable when the chain is compromised.

Ideological interpretations of property often ignore this distinction. They focus on origins, abstractions, or moral claims while bypassing the actual mechanism that determines enforceability.

Courts do not adjudicate beliefs about ownership.

They adjudicate competing interests as reflected in records. A clean chain does not guarantee the absence of conflict, but it provides a stable foundation for resolving it.

One reason chain of title is frequently misunderstood is that it operates quietly. When it works, nothing happens. Transactions proceed. Ownership is recognized. Life continues. When it fails, the consequences can be sudden and severe. Sales collapse. Financing evaporates. Disputes surface that cannot be resolved by reference to a single document or declaration. At that point, ideology offers no remedy. Only the record matters.

Another source of confusion lies in the assumption that chain of title is merely historical.

In reality, it is dynamic.

Every new transaction becomes part of the chain.

Every recorded interest modifies it.

Ownership is not a static condition established once and preserved indefinitely. It is maintained through ongoing compliance with recording requirements and legal formalities. Neglecting that maintenance does not invalidate ownership immediately, but it introduces weakness.

Ideological narratives often appeal because they promise shortcuts. They suggest that a single insight, document, or assertion can bypass complexity. The chain of title offers no shortcuts.

It demands consistency. Each link must be capable of standing on its own, yet also fit seamlessly into the whole.

Weakness in one link does not necessarily destroy the chain, but it creates points of attack.

Courts are acutely aware of this structure. When disputes arise, judges do not ask which party holds the most compelling theory of ownership.

They ask which party can demonstrate continuity of interest through recognized records. Assertions untethered from the chain are treated as speculative, regardless of how confidently they are presented.
Understanding the primacy of chain of title reframes how property security is assessed.
It shifts attention away from dramatic claims and toward practical realities. It also explains why some arguments that sound persuasive in online forums fail decisively in legal settings. They do not engage with the system that determines outcomes.
Strength in property ownership comes from alignment with that system.
The chain of title is its backbone.
When it is intact, ownership is defensible.
When it is fractured, even the most passionate assertions struggle to survive scrutiny.
Recognizing this does not require abandoning interest in foundational documents or historical context. It requires understanding where real leverage exists. In property law, leverage flows through records, not rhetoric. The chain is where authority accumulates, erodes, and ultimately reveals itself.
That realization leads naturally to a more detailed examination of how chains weaken—not in theory, but in practice.

Typical Defects, Gaps, and Breaks Explained

Chains of title do not fail all at once. They weaken gradually, often invisibly, until a transaction or dispute exposes the underlying problem. These weaknesses are rarely dramatic.
They arise from human error, administrative oversight, incomplete records, or changes in law that outpace documentation. Understanding how defects form requires abandoning the idea that title problems are rare anomalies.
They are common enough that entire industries exist to manage them.
A defect occurs when an interest in property is unclear, improperly documented, or legally questionable. Some defects are minor and easily cured. Others are structural and persist across decades. The distinction matters because not all defects carry the same risk.
What unites them is their effect on continuity.

They disrupt the narrative of ownership that the chain is meant to tell.

Gaps often occur when a transfer is not properly recorded. A deed may have been executed but never filed. A probate proceeding may have resolved ownership without resulting in a clear conveyance. Over time, these omissions compound.

Later transactions rely on assumptions rather than verified records. The chain appears intact until examined closely.

Breaks are more severe. They occur when the documented history fails to establish a clear line from one owner to the next. This can happen through invalid deeds, conflicting claims, or unresolved interests.

A break does not necessarily mean ownership is lost, but it does mean it is contestable. Contestability introduces risk, particularly in adversarial contexts. To make these categories concrete, consider some of the defects that title examiners encounter regularly.

A deed signed by a married person without spousal joinder, in a state that requires it, creates a defect.

A foreclosure conducted without proper notice to all parties with an interest leaves the title clouded.

An estate that passes through intestacy without a probate proceeding leaves no recorded conveyance to the heirs.

A divorce decree that awards property to one spouse but is never reflected in a recorded deed creates a gap between the court's order and the public record.

A legal description that references a survey plat which was later amended creates ambiguity about what was actually conveyed.

A deed executed by someone who had already conveyed the property to another party creates competing claims.

Each of these situations arises from ordinary life, not from conspiracy, and each can compromise the chain if left unresolved.

Some defects arise from ambiguity.

Legal descriptions may be vague or inconsistent. Boundary lines may shift due to surveys conducted under different standards. Names may change, be misspelled, or be duplicated across generations.

These issues seem trivial until they intersect with enforcement or transfer.

Other defects stem from timing. Interests created out of sequence can disrupt priority. A lien recorded late may nevertheless assert priority due to statutory provisions.

A release may be executed but not recorded promptly, leaving the record misleading. Time matters in property law, not abstractly, but procedurally.

What makes these defects dangerous is not their existence, but their invisibility. A homeowner may live on a property for decades without encountering any issue. That experience reinforces the belief that ownership is unassailable. When a problem finally surfaces, it often does so under pressure, when options are limited.

Courts do not treat defects as moral failures. They treat them as factual conditions. The question is not why a defect exists, but what legal effect it has. Ideological explanations are irrelevant. The record either supports continuity or it does not.

Understanding defects also clarifies why reliance on a single document is risky. Ownership is not proven by any one instrument. It is demonstrated by coherence across instruments.

When coherence breaks down, even valid documents can lose effectiveness.

The existence of defects does not automatically invalidate ownership, but it shifts the burden. Where the chain is clean, ownership is presumed. Where it is broken, ownership must be defended. That defense depends on evidence, not assertion.

Recognizing typical defects demystifies title risk. It replaces vague anxiety with identifiable conditions.

That clarity allows homeowners to assess exposure realistically rather than reacting to exaggerated claims or false assurances.

As attention turns from abstract weakness to concrete encumbrances, another category of interests comes into focus—interests that do not break the chain, but shape its operation.

Liens, Easements, Reservations, and Restrictions

Not all interests that affect property ownership weaken the chain of title. Many coexist with it, shaping how ownership is exercised without undermining its legitimacy.

Liens, easements, reservations, and restrictions are among the most common of these interests. They are often misunderstood because they feel like intrusions, yet they are integral to how property functions within a legal system.

A lien represents a claim against property to secure an obligation. It does not transfer ownership, but it conditions it.
The existence of a lien means that another party has a legally recognized interest that can, under certain circumstances, be enforced against the property.
This enforcement does not arise from ideology or assertion; it arises from compliance with statutory procedures.
Easements operate differently.
They grant limited rights of use to parties other than the owner. An easement does not diminish ownership, but it constrains exclusivity. A driveway easement, utility access, or right-of-way alters how land can be used without challenging who owns it.
These interests are often created intentionally, yet over time they can be forgotten, misunderstood, or disputed.
Reservations and restrictions further complicate the picture.
A reservation retains certain rights for the grantor at the time of conveyance. Restrictions impose conditions on use, often to maintain uniformity or protect shared interests. These limitations are not defects.
They are part of the ownership package as defined by law. Among the most consequential reservations in American property law are mineral reservations. As discussed in Chapter 2, many land patents — particularly those issued under the Stock Raising Homestead Act of 1916 — reserved all mineral rights to the United States.
When those minerals were later conveyed or leased, a "severed mineral estate" was created: the surface owner holds the surf ace rights, while a separate party holds the mineral rights beneath.
The mineral estate is generally considered the "dominant" estate, meaning the mineral owner has an implied right of reasonable access across the surface to extract the minerals.
This severance can persist indefinitely through the chain of title. Similarly, water rights in western states governed by the prior appropriation doctrine are often separate from surface ownership and may trace back to the original patent or to rights established independently of it.
A property owner who does not investigate these reservations may discover, too late, that the most valuable subsurface interests were never part of what they acquired.
What unites these interests is their visibility within the chain of title. When properly recorded, they do not weaken ownership; they define it.

Problems arise when they are ignored or misunderstood. A homeowner who assumes absolute freedom may violate restrictions unintentionally. A buyer unaware of an easement may feel blindsided later.

In both cases, the issue is not the existence of the interest, but the failure to recognize it.

Ideological narratives often frame these interests as evidence that ownership is incomplete or illusory. This framing misrepresents their function.

Ownership has always existed alongside shared rights and obligations. These interests do not negate ownership; they enable coexistence.

From a legal perspective, liens, easements, reservations, and restrictions are not anomalies.

They are expected components of the property system. Courts enforce them because they are part of the documented record. Ignoring them does not remove their effect; it simply increases exposure.

Understanding these interests requires a shift away from viewing ownership as domination and toward viewing it as participation in a regulated environment. Participation does not imply weakness. It implies recognition.

What Land Patents Do and Do Not Fix in a Broken Chain

When questions about the chain of title arise, land patents are often invoked as a kind of corrective force.

The logic feels intuitive: if the chain is weak, return to the beginning. If later links are questionable, rely on the original grant.

This line of thinking is understandable, especially in an environment where land patents are frequently described as ultimate proof of ownership.

Yet this intuition misunderstands how chains break, how they are repaired, and what role historical instruments actually play in that process.

A chain of title does not function like a rope that can be reattached at the top once it frays at the bottom. It functions more like a ledger. Each entry builds on the last, and each must be intelligible within the same accounting system.

When later entries are missing, unclear, or conflicting, pointing to the first entry does not reconcile the discrepancy. The problem is not where the chain began; it is how it continued.

Land patents establish that land was lawfully conveyed from a sovereign authority into private ownership. That fact is rarely in dispute. In most cases, no one challenges whether land was once part of the public domain or whether a patent was properly issued.

The vulnerability arises much later, when subsequent transfers, encumbrances, or recordings introduce uncertainty. Those uncertainties cannot be resolved by reasserting origin. They must be addressed where they occur.

One common misconception is that a land patent can override missing or defective transfers. If a deed was never recorded, or if an interest was conveyed improperly, some assume that referencing the patent restores clarity.

In reality, the patent predates the defect and therefore cannot cure it.

The defect exists within the chain as it developed, not at its inception.

Courts evaluate the chain as a whole, not as a series of isolated moments. The legal system provides specific tools for repairing broken chains, and none of them involve invoking a land patent.

A quiet title action asks a court to determine ownership and eliminate competing claims. A curative statute in many states automatically corrects minor defects — such as missing acknowledgments or defective notarizations — after a specified period.

A corrective deed or confirmatory deed can fix errors in a prior conveyance when the original parties are available and willing. In some states, an affidavit of heirship can bridge gaps left by estates that passed without probate.

Adverse possession, where applicable, can establish ownership through continuous, open, hostile, and exclusive possession for a period defined by state law — typically ranging from five years in California to twenty-one years in Pennsylvania. Each of these tools operates within the recording and judicial system. Each addresses a specific type of break. None of them rely on the age or origin of the original conveyance.

Another misunderstanding involves priority. Some believe that because the patent came first, it outranks all later interests. Priority in property law does not work that way.

Priority is determined by statutory rules governing recording, notice, and timing. A lien recorded decades after a patent can still have priority over other interests if the law so provides. The patent does not displace those rules; it operates beneath them.

This distinction becomes critical in disputes involving enforcement. When a lienholder, taxing authority, or other claimant asserts an interest, the question is not whether the land was originally patented, but whether the claimant's interest was created and recorded in compliance with current law.

A land patent does not negate that compliance. It does not invalidate enforcement mechanisms. Courts do not view patents as shields against obligations that arose long after the land left public ownership.

There is also a tendency to treat patents as tools for rewriting the record. Some homeowners attempt to record documents referencing the original patent in hopes of "correcting" perceived defects. Recording such documents does not alter the existing chain.

It adds a new document to the record, but it does not remove or repair earlier inconsistencies. In some cases, it introduces additional ambiguity by layering unsupported claims onto an already complex history.

The legal system distinguishes sharply between evidence of origin and evidence of continuity. Land patents serve the former function. They demonstrate how ownership began.

They do not demonstrate how ownership was maintained. When continuity is disrupted—through unclear transfers, unresolved interests, or recording failures—the remedy lies in addressing those disruptions directly, not in invoking a document that predates them. This is not a matter of courts being hostile to land patents.

It is a matter of courts adhering to the logic of the system they are tasked with administering. Property law depends on predictability. Allowing historical documents to retroactively override later developments would undermine that predictability.

It would create uncertainty not only for individual owners, but for everyone who relies on the integrity of recorded interests.

Understanding what land patents do not fix also helps explain why they sometimes appear to work in narrow contexts. In cases where a dispute involves the legitimacy of initial conveyance—such as conflicting historical claims—a patent may be relevant evidence. These situations are rare. In the vast majority of modern disputes, the issue is not whether the land was lawfully conveyed out of public ownership, but whether later interests were properly created, recorded, and enforced.

When patents are applied outside their proper scope, the risk is not merely theoretical. Homeowners may delay addressing real defects while focusing on symbolic solutions. They may reject practical remedies in favor of assertions that lack legal effect. By the time the misunderstanding becomes clear, options may be limited.

What land patents can do is provide historical grounding. They can clarify whether land entered private ownership through federal conveyance. They can support research into early ownership patterns. They can help explain why certain records exist and others do not. Used in this way, they enhance understanding.

What they cannot do is repair breaks that occur later in the chain. They cannot substitute for missing deeds, cure invalid transfers, or extinguish properly recorded interests.

Expecting them to do so assigns them a role they were never designed to play.

The strength of a chain of title lies in its internal coherence. Repairing that coherence requires working within the same system that evaluates it. That system values clarity, continuity, and compliance. Historical documents contribute context, not correction.

Chapter 6 – Risk Zones: Where Land Patent Claims Commonly Fail

Taxation Myths and Zoning Misconceptions

Few areas generate more confident misinformation than property taxation and zoning. They touch daily life, evoke strong emotional responses, and are often experienced as impositions rather than as legal mechanisms. When land patents enter the discussion, these feelings intensify.

Taxation and zoning become framed not as regulatory realities, but as evidence that ownership is somehow incomplete or compromised. This framing creates one of the most common and dangerous risk zones for homeowners exploring land patent claims.

The myth usually begins with a simple premise: if land was once conveyed into private ownership through a sovereign act, ongoing taxation must be illegitimate.

From there, zoning restrictions are portrayed as overreach, incompatible with "true" ownership. These ideas gain traction because they resonate emotionally. Taxes feel coercive. Zoning feels arbitrary. The promise that a historical document could dissolve both is appealing. It is also legally unsound.

Property taxation does not arise from how land entered private ownership. It arises from jurisdiction.

Once land becomes privately owned within a state, it becomes part of that state's taxable base. This is not a loophole or a modern invention. It is a foundational feature of how governments fund services that make private ownership viable: courts, infrastructure, emergency services, and recordkeeping itself.

The power to tax real property is among the oldest and most firmly established of all governmental powers. It derives from the sovereign's inherent authority, delegated by state constitutions to local governments. The U.S. Supreme Court has never held that a land patent creates an exemption from property taxation, and no federal statute provides such an exemption.

To the contrary, the Court confirmed in McCulloch v. Maryland, 17 U.S. 316 (1819), the principle that the power to tax is fundamental to governance, and in Brushaber v. Union Pacific R.R., 240 U.S. 1 (1916), it upheld the broad reach of legislative taxing authority.

Taxation is tied to the presence of property within a governing authority, not to the language of an original conveyance.
Land patents do not alter this relationship.
They do not remove property from the tax rolls.
They do not convert private land into a special category immune from assessment.
Courts have consistently treated attempts to avoid taxation through patent-based arguments as misunderstandings of how taxing authority operates.
When such arguments are raised, they are typically dismissed quickly, not because taxation is beyond challenge, but because the challenge is misdirected. The practical consequences of nonpayment are severe and escalate predictably. Unpaid property taxes accrue penalties and interest.
After a defined period — which varies by state but typically ranges from one to five years — the taxing authority may initiate a tax lien sale or a tax deed sale, ultimately resulting in loss of the property. A homeowner who stops paying taxes based on a patent theory does not pause the tax clock; the clock continues whether or not the homeowner acknowledges it.
Zoning misconceptions follow a similar pattern. Zoning is often portrayed as a violation of ownership rather than as a condition of it.
The belief is that if land was originally granted without restrictions, modern limitations must be invalid. This reasoning ignores how zoning authority developed.
The constitutionality of zoning was settled by the U.S. Supreme Court in Village of Euclid v. Ambler Realty Co., 272 U.S. 365 (1926), which upheld comprehensive zoning as a valid exercise of the state's police power. Nearly a century later, that holding remains good law. Every state has enabling legislation that delegates zoning authority to municipalities and counties.
Zoning does not retroactively alter ownership; it regulates use within a community. It applies uniformly, regardless of origin, because its purpose is coordination, not confiscation. Land patents do not exempt property from zoning laws. They do not grant unilateral discretion over land use. They do not override ordinances enacted under state authority. When homeowners attempt to assert patent-based exemptions from zoning requirements, they often discover that enforcement proceeds regardless of those assertions.

The resulting penalties can escalate quickly, especially when noncompliance is prolonged.

What makes taxation and zoning myths particularly risky is that they encourage inaction.

A homeowner convinced that taxes are illegitimate may stop paying them.

A homeowner convinced that zoning does not apply may ignore enforcement notices.

These decisions are often framed as principled stands. Legally, they are treated as defaults.

By the time the misunderstanding becomes clear, the financial and legal consequences may be severe.

Another danger lies in selective interpretation. Advocates of patent-based exemptions often cite fragments of historical language without acknowledging the broader legal context.

They conflate opposition to taxation with immunity from it.

They frame zoning as tyranny rather than as a negotiated expression of public authority. These narratives thrive online but collapse under legal scrutiny.

Understanding the risk here requires separating frustration from analysis. Disliking taxes does not make them unlawful. Disagreeing with zoning does not negate its enforceability. Land patents do not transform those disagreements into legal defenses. Acting as though they do introduces exposure rather than protection.

When homeowners encounter claims suggesting otherwise, the appropriate response is not fear or dismissal, but careful evaluation.

Ask what authority enforces the obligation.

Ask whether courts recognize the exemption being claimed.

Ask whether similar arguments have succeeded under comparable circumstances.

These questions tend to reveal the gap between rhetoric and reality.

Taxation and zoning are not peripheral issues. They are central to property governance. Misunderstanding their relationship to land patents places homeowners in direct conflict with authorities that have clear enforcement power. That conflict rarely ends in favor of the homeowner.

As attention shifts from regulatory obligations to financial enforcement, another high-risk area comes into view—one where consequences are often irreversible.

Foreclosure Claims That Do Not Hold Up in Court

Foreclosure is where theory meets consequence. It is the point at which misunderstandings about property law stop being abstract and become immediate.

For this reason, foreclosure-related claims involving land patents are among the most consequential—and most frequently unsuccessful—applications of patent-based arguments.

The central misconception is the belief that a land patent nullifies a lender's interest.

The reasoning often goes like this: if the land was originally granted free of encumbrance, and if a patent represents ultimate ownership, then no later financial instrument can legitimately attach to it. This reasoning overlooks a fundamental fact: lenders do not rely on origin. They rely on contracts.

A mortgage or deed of trust is not imposed by force. It is entered into voluntarily. When a homeowner signs a financing agreement, they grant a security interest in the property. That interest is enforceable because it arises from consent and is recognized by law. The existence of a land patent does not invalidate that consent, nor does it negate the agreement that followed.

Courts view foreclosure through this contractual lens.

The question is not whether the homeowner holds ultimate ownership in some abstract sense.

The question is whether a valid agreement exists and whether its terms have been breached. Patent-based arguments that ignore this contractual reality fail because they do not address the basis of enforcement.

The Supreme Court affirmed the legitimacy of foreclosure sales in BFP v. Resolution Trust Corp., 511 U.S. 531 (1994), holding that a foreclosure sale conducted in compliance with state law is presumptively valid. The Court's reasoning centered on the contractual and statutory framework governing mortgage enforcement — not on the historical origin of the land.

It is worth noting that foreclosure procedures themselves vary by state. Roughly half the states use judicial foreclosure, requiring the lender to file a lawsuit and obtain a court order before selling the property.

The other half permit nonjudicial foreclosure through a power-of-sale clause in the deed of trust, allowing the sale to proceed without court involvement.

In judicial foreclosure states, a homeowner has the opportunity to raise defenses in court — but those defenses must be grounded in contract law, procedural requirements, or statutory protections, not in historical patent claims.

In nonjudicial foreclosure states, the window for contesting the sale is even narrower, governed by strict statutory timelines. In either system, time spent pursuing patent-based arguments is time not spent exploring defenses that might actually apply: improper notice, failure to satisfy conditions precedent, violations of the Servicemembers Civil Relief Act, or errors in the assignment of the mortgage.

Another common foreclosure-related claim involves jurisdiction. Some argue that because land patents originated federally, state courts lack authority to adjudicate foreclosure actions.

This argument misunderstands both jurisdiction and the nature of foreclosure proceedings. State courts enforce contracts, not conveyances. They have authority over property within their territory precisely because state law governs private property relationships.

When patent-based jurisdictional challenges are raised, courts routinely reject them. Jurisdiction is established by statute, geography, and subject matter, not by historical origin. Attempting to remove foreclosure proceedings from state court based on patent arguments rarely succeeds and often delays resolution in ways that increase costs.

Some homeowners also believe that recording documents referencing a land patent will cloud title in a way that blocks foreclosure. This belief confuses disruption with defense.

Creating confusion in the record does not eliminate a lender's interest. It may delay proceedings, but it does not change the underlying obligation. Courts and lenders are equipped to cut through such filings and proceed with enforcement. What makes foreclosure claims particularly dangerous is timing. Foreclosure timelines are unforgiving. Deadlines matter. Remedies narrow quickly. When homeowners rely on arguments that do not hold up, they may miss opportunities to pursue options that could actually mitigate harm.

Those options include loan modification, forbearance agreements, short sale, deed in lieu of foreclosure, and — in appropriate cases — bankruptcy, which triggers an automatic stay under 11 U.S.C. § 362. Each of these operates within the legal system. None of them require a land patent.By the time the argument fails, alternatives may be gone.

Courts do not treat foreclosure as a philosophical dispute.

They treat it as a process governed by statute and contract. Arguments that do not engage with those elements are sidelined. Judges may acknowledge the existence of a patent, then return immediately to the agreement that created the lender's rights.

Understanding this judicial posture is essential.

It explains why confidence alone does not protect against foreclosure. It also explains why patent-based defenses are often dismissed without extensive analysis. From the court's perspective, the issue is settled by the contract and the law governing it.

Foreclosure is a high-stakes environment.

Entering it armed with arguments that courts consistently reject increases risk rather than reducing it. That risk is not theoretical. It is measured in lost property, damaged credit, and prolonged legal exposure.

As patterns emerge in how patent-based claims fail, certain warning signs become visible. These signs are not always obvious at first, but recognizing them early can prevent deeper entanglement.

Red Flags That Signal Legal Exposure

Legal exposure rarely announces itself directly. It develops through a series of small decisions, each justified by confidence, urgency, or belief. In the context of land patent claims, certain patterns recur often enough to be considered warning signs.

These red flags do not guarantee failure, but they indicate heightened risk—particularly when they appear together.

One of the earliest signals is the reliance on absolute language. Claims framed in terms of "always," "never," or "automatically" should prompt caution. Property law is conditional by nature. Outcomes depend on jurisdiction, timing, and procedure.

Assertions that bypass those variables often lack legal grounding.

When advice discourages nuance, it is usually because nuance undermines the claim being made.

Another red flag appears when legal authority is described as irrelevant or illegitimate. Statements suggesting that courts are corrupt, ignorant, or powerless serve a psychological function.

They preempt accountability. If the system is framed as broken, failure can be attributed to bias rather than to flawed reasoning. This framing is emotionally reassuring, but legally dangerous.

Courts are not optional participants in property disputes; they are the forum in which those disputes are resolved. Isolation is another indicator.

When homeowners are encouraged to distrust professionals universally, to avoid neutral advice, or to rely exclusively on a single source of information, exposure increases.

Legal systems are complex precisely because they involve multiple perspectives. Advice that discourages verification or consultation often does so to protect the narrative, not the homeowner.

A related warning sign involves financial exploitation. Some promoters of land patent strategies charge substantial fees for document preparation, "patent updating" services, or seminar attendance.

These services typically produce documents that have no legal effect. A homeowner who pays hundreds or thousands of dollars for a "updated land patent" or a "declaration of allodial title" has purchased paper, not protection.

There is no recognized legal procedure for "updating" or "bringing forward" a land patent. If someone charges money for such a service, that alone should raise serious concerns.

Procedural shortcuts also signal risk. Claims that a single filing, affidavit, or notice will fundamentally alter legal relationships underestimate the procedural rigor of property law. Rights are rarely created or extinguished through unilateral action.

When strategies emphasize form over substance, or paperwork over compliance, they tend to collapse under scrutiny.

Timing-related red flags deserve particular attention. Advice that urges immediate action without regard for deadlines, jurisdiction, or consequence often prioritizes momentum over accuracy. In legal matters, haste is rarely neutral. It magnifies errors and reduces options.

Another warning sign is the dismissal of recorded interests as mere technicalities.

Liens, assessments, and restrictions are not technicalities; they are enforceable claims. Treating them as distractions or illusions does not neutralize them. It delays engagement until enforcement becomes unavoidable.
Perhaps the most subtle red flag is emotional reinforcement. Advice that consistently validates frustration, anger, or fear without introducing restraint often trades clarity for comfort.
Comfort does not protect property. Understanding does.
Recognizing these signals requires stepping back from the immediate appeal of certainty.
It requires asking uncomfortable questions about enforceability, precedent, and consequence. That questioning is not disloyalty to the idea of ownership; it is loyalty to its preservation.
Legal exposure thrives where belief outruns verification.
The earlier that imbalance is recognized, the easier it is to correct.
Risk zones do not exist because homeowners ask questions.
They exist because answers are accepted without scrutiny.

Why Paper Filings Alone Rarely Change Outcomes

One of the most persistent beliefs surrounding land patent strategies is the idea that action itself creates authority.
File the right document.
Record the right notice.
Use the correct language.
Once the paperwork is in place, the thinking goes, the legal reality must adjust accordingly. This belief is not unique to land patents, but it finds particularly fertile ground there because of the historical weight and formal tone associated with old conveyance documents.
The danger lies in mistaking movement for effectiveness.
Paper filings feel powerful because they are tangible. They can be printed, stamped, recorded, and referenced. They create the impression that something has been done, that a line has been crossed from uncertainty into control. In legal systems, however, paperwork is not a source of authority. It is a method of expressing authority that already exists. When filings attempt to create authority rather than reflect it, they rarely alter outcomes.
Recording systems are designed to give notice, not to adjudicate disputes. When a document is recorded, it becomes visible to the public.

That visibility does not validate its contents. It does not confer legal weight beyond what the underlying law already recognizes.

A recorder's office does not assess legal merit; it performs an administrative function. Confusing administrative acceptance with legal endorsement is one of the most common and costly errors homeowners make.

Courts are keenly aware of this distinction. When disputes arise, judges do not ask whether a document was recorded. They ask what legal interest the document represents and whether that interest is recognized by law.

A filing that asserts exemption, supremacy, or immunity without statutory or contractual support is treated as an assertion, not a fact. Its presence in the record does not elevate it beyond scrutiny. Moreover, recording unsupported claims against another party's property can give rise to a cause of action for slander of title — a tort in which a party records a false claim that impairs the marketability of someone else's title.

A successful slander-of-title claim can result in an award of damages, attorney's fees, and in some jurisdictions, punitive damages. Filing documents is not a consequence-free activity.

Another misconception is that volume compensates for weakness. Some homeowners are advised to file multiple documents affidavits, notices, declarations—under the assumption that repetition creates legitimacy. In practice, excessive filings often have the opposite effect. They signal misunderstanding, not authority. Courts and opposing parties do not become overwhelmed by paperwork; they categorize it.

Unsupported filings are grouped together and addressed collectively, often with little patience.

There is also a tendency to treat historical language as legally operative simply because it sounds authoritative.

Quoting phrases from patents or early statutes and embedding them into modern filings does not transplant their original force. Legal language derives its effect from context, not from tone. A sentence that carried weight in one century does not automatically carry it in another.

Courts interpret language through current legal frameworks, not through rhetorical reverence. Paper filings also fail to change outcomes because they do not alter relationships. Property disputes revolve around enforceable interests: obligations, rights, priorities. Those interests arise from law, contract, and compliance.

Filing a document does not extinguish a debt. It does not dissolve a lien.

It does not negate jurisdiction.

Without altering the underlying relationship, the dispute remains unchanged regardless of how many documents are recorded. This reality becomes especially clear in enforcement contexts.

Tax authorities do not halt collection because a notice has been filed.

Lenders do not abandon foreclosure because an affidavit challenges their authority.

Zoning officials do not suspend enforcement because a declaration asserts exemption. Enforcement bodies act based on statutes and orders, not on unilateral claims.

Another overlooked aspect is that filings can create unintended consequences.

Recording documents that assert unsupported claims may cloud title temporarily, but that cloud does not function as protection.

It can complicate future transactions, invite legal challenge, or trigger corrective action. In some jurisdictions, a pattern of filing frivolous or fraudulent documents can itself become the basis for criminal prosecution. California Penal Code § 115 makes it a felony to knowingly file a false or forged instrument for recording. Colorado's C.R.S. § 38-35-109 provides civil remedies against persons who file fraudulent liens or encumbrances.

In some jurisdictions, a pattern of filing frivolous or fraudulent documents can itself become the basis for criminal prosecution. California Penal Code § 115 makes it a felony to knowingly file a false or forged instrument for recording.

Colorado's C.R.S. § 38-35-109 provides civil remedies against persons who file fraudulent liens or encumbrances. Several states have enacted specific "vexatious litigant" statutes that restrict future court access for individuals who repeatedly file frivolous actions.In some cases, such filings are treated as frivolous or obstructive, increasing scrutiny rather than reducing it.

The belief in paper-based solutions often stems from frustration with systems that feel inaccessible or unresponsive. Filing documents becomes a way to assert presence, to demand recognition. That impulse is understandable. The legal system, however, does not respond to demands. It responds to arguments grounded in law and supported by evidence.

There is also a psychological component at play. Filing documents provides a sense of agency. It replaces waiting with action. When faced with uncertainty or threat, action feels safer than restraint. Yet action without alignment can be more dangerous than inaction. It creates false confidence and delays engagement with strategies that might actually affect outcomes.

Courts often articulate this distinction implicitly. Opinions rejecting paper-based strategies emphasize substance over form. They focus on whether the filer has addressed the legal basis of the opposing claim. When the answer is no, the filings are treated as noise rather than signal.

This does not mean that documentation is unimportant. Documentation is central to property law. The difference lies in purpose. Documents that reflect valid transactions, comply with statutory requirements, and integrate into the existing legal framework carry weight. Documents that attempt to override that framework do not.

Understanding why paper filings alone rarely change outcomes reframes how homeowners approach risk.

It shifts the focus from producing documents to understanding relationships. It replaces the question "What can I file?" with "What authority governs this situation?" That shift is subtle but decisive.

Chapter 7 – When Land Patents May Have Limited Practical Value

Situations Where Patents Offer Historical Clarity Only

There are moments in property research when a land patent proves genuinely useful—not because it alters present conditions, but because it explains how those conditions came to exist.
In these situations, the patent functions as a historical anchor. It provides orientation. It answers questions about origin, legitimacy of early conveyance, and the pathway by which land moved from public control into private hands. What it does not do is change the legal environment in which the property currently operates.
This distinction matters because clarity and leverage are not the same thing. Historical clarity can be intellectually satisfying and practically informative without carrying direct legal force. Problems arise when these two are conflated—when understanding is mistaken for authority.

One common situation where land patents offer value without power is genealogical or archival research. Homeowners tracing how land entered a family's possession often encounter gaps in early records. A patent can confirm that the land was lawfully granted and identify the original recipient. That confirmation resolves questions about legitimacy that might otherwise linger. It does not, however, resolve questions about present-day rights, obligations, or disputes.

Another context involves disputes over early boundaries or naming inconsistencies. Older conveyances often used landmarks that no longer exist or descriptions that evolved over time.
A land patent can help establish the starting reference point from which later descriptions developed. This can assist surveyors, historians, or legal professionals in reconstructing intent. The patent serves as a reference frame, not as an override.
There are also cases where property owners encounter claims suggesting that land was never properly conveyed out of public ownership. In such cases, a patent can be dispositive. It demonstrates that the transfer occurred under recognized authority. Once that question is settled, however, the patent's role diminishes. It does not govern what happened afterward.

In rural areas or regions with complex settlement histories, patents can clarify why certain parcels are subject to unique reservations or exclusions. Mineral rights, water rights, or rights-of-way often trace back to early conveyances.

Understanding the original grant helps explain why these interests exist. It does not eliminate them.

In Michigan, courts have recognized a narrow but genuine role for land patents in establishing ownership of submerged lands — situations where the original patent description included areas that later became lake bottom due to rising water levels.

The Michigan Supreme Court held that the patent's legal description controlled ownership of the submerged parcel, preserving the surface owner's rights against the state's navigable-waters claim. This is one of the few modern contexts in which a patent's specific language directly determined a property outcome. But even here, the patent functioned as evidence of what was originally conveyed not as a source of immunity from regulation.

The value of historical clarity lies in context. It helps homeowners understand the shape of their ownership, the reasons certain limitations exist, and the origins of recorded interests.

This understanding can reduce confusion and prevent misinterpretation. It can also inform better decision-making by aligning expectations with reality.

Problems emerge when historical clarity is mistaken for present authority. A patent does not freeze property law at the moment of issuance. It does not preserve a legal environment that no longer exists. It does not suspend the evolution of governance, regulation, or private ordering. Treating it as such introduces distortion rather than insight.

The temptation to elevate historical documents arises partly from frustration with complexity. Modern property law feels layered, indirect, and procedural. Historical documents feel direct. They speak in absolute terms. They appear to offer certainty. That appearance is misleading. Their certainty belongs to their time, not to ours.

Recognizing situations where patents offer clarity without leverage allows homeowners to use them appropriately. They become tools for understanding rather than weapons for confrontation. This shift in posture reduces risk and increases coherence.

When patents are placed in their proper role, they enhance knowledge without distorting expectations. They illuminate history without claiming authority over the present. That restraint preserves their usefulness.

As attention moves from understanding origins to navigating current conditions, it becomes evident that other tools often provide more effective protection.

Cases Where Other Legal Tools Are More Effective

Modern property ownership operates within a dense network of legal mechanisms designed to manage risk, resolve disputes, and allocate responsibility. These mechanisms exist precisely because ownership is not static. It is exposed to change, conflict, and uncertainty. In this environment, effectiveness is measured not by symbolism, but by enforceability.

The following comparison illustrates why modern tools consistently outperform patent-based strategies when addressing common property problems:

Problem	Land Patent	Effective Tool
Defect in chain of title	Cannot cure post-patent defects	Quiet title action; corrective deed; curative statute
Unknown prior claims	No protection against undiscovered interests	Title insurance (owner's policy)
Boundary dispute with neighbor	Patent description may be outdated or imprecise	Survey; boundary line agreement; quiet title action
Estate planning / inheritance	Does not guide succession	Trust; will; transfer-on-death deed (where available)
Lien or encumbrance	Cannot extinguish valid liens	Payoff; negotiation; lien release; bankruptcy
Unclear mineral rights	May clarify original reservation	Mineral title search; quiet title; dormant mineral act
Tax delinquency	No exemption from taxation	Payment plan; tax abatement; appeal of assessment
Zoning violation	No exemption from zoning	Variance; special use permit; rezoning petition

There are many situations where invoking a land patent adds little value compared to other available tools. Title insurance is one such example.

It addresses defects, gaps, and unknown claims in a way that historical documents cannot. It does not rely on origin. It responds to risk. When problems arise, it provides a pathway to resolution rather than an argument about authority.

Title insurance comes in two forms: an owner's policy, which protects the buyer, and a lender's policy, which protects the mortgage holder.

Policies issued under American Land Title Association (ALTA) standards are the industry norm.

An owner's policy is a one-time purchase that remains in effect for as long as the insured or their heirs hold an interest in the property. It covers losses from covered title defects, pays for legal defense when covered claims arise, and is backed by a regulated insurer — none of which a land patent can provide.

Corrective instruments offer another illustration. When errors appear in recorded documents—misspelled names, inconsistent descriptions, missing acknowledgments—there are established procedures to cure them.

These procedures operate within the recording system. They engage directly with the source of weakness. Referencing a patent does not correct a defective deed. Executing a corrective instrument does.

Estate planning tools also demonstrate the limits of patent-based thinking. Trusts, wills, and transfer-on-death mechanisms manage continuity across generations.

They reduce ambiguity and prevent disputes. A land patent does not replace these instruments. It does not guide inheritance. It does not prevent fragmentation of interests.

Relying on it in place of proper planning often leaves families vulnerable. Transfer-on-death deeds (TODDs), now authorized in approximately thirty states under various names, allow property to pass to a named beneficiary without probate.

They are revocable during the owner's lifetime and take effect only at death.

They cost very little to prepare and record.

They accomplish in a single page what no patent theory can deliver: a clean, legally recognized transfer that avoids the delays and costs of probate.

In disputes involving neighbors, easements, or shared access, negotiated agreements and court orders provide resolution. These outcomes depend on current law and mutual recognition. Historical conveyance documents rarely influence them directly. Attempting to inject patent-based arguments into such disputes often complicates matters without advancing resolution.

Financial exposure is another area where other tools dominate. Liens, assessments, and obligations arise from contracts and statutes. Addressing them requires compliance, negotiation, or litigation. Historical origin does not dissolve these relationships.

Practical tools engage with the mechanisms that created the exposure.

The effectiveness of these tools lies in their alignment with the system that enforces property rights. They are recognized, predictable, and adaptable.

They do not promise immunity; they offer process. That process may be imperfect, but it is operative.

Choosing effective tools over symbolic ones requires humility. It means accepting that ownership involves participation rather than exemption.

It means recognizing that strength comes from engagement, not withdrawal. This perspective is less emotionally satisfying than narratives of absolute control, but it produces better outcomes.

The danger of overvaluing land patents is not that they are meaningless, but that they can distract from solutions that actually work.

When attention is fixed on asserting origin, opportunities to manage present risk may be missed.

Understanding which tools are effective in which contexts is a mark of maturity in property ownership. It reflects a shift from seeking validation to seeking stability.

That shift becomes especially important when pressure increases—when disputes escalate, enforcement looms, or timelines compress. Under those conditions, strategies that do not produce results quickly lose their appeal.

When homeowners insist on using tools unsuited to the problem, the consequences can be severe. That insistence often arises from the belief that the tool carries inherent power.

When that belief is challenged, frustration grows.

This frustration sets the stage for the next risk: forcing a strategy beyond its natural limits.

Why Forcing a Patent Strategy Can Backfire

Forcing a strategy is rarely a conscious decision. It usually emerges gradually, as investment deepens and alternatives feel like concessions. In the context of land patents, this pattern is particularly pronounced.

Once a homeowner commits emotionally or intellectually to the idea that a patent should solve a problem, evidence to the contrary can feel threatening. Persistence becomes a virtue. Doubt becomes betrayal. This dynamic creates conditions where backfire is not only possible, but likely.

One way forced strategies backfire is through escalation. When initial assertions are ignored or rejected, the response is often to intensify them. More documents are filed. Language becomes stronger. Claims broaden. What began as inquiry transforms into confrontation. Each escalation increases visibility without increasing legal traction. Courts and agencies interpret this pattern predictably. Repetition without substance is not persuasive; it is diagnostic. It signals misunderstanding of process. It invites scrutiny rather than accommodation. Once a pattern is established, future filings may be viewed through that lens, reducing their credibility regardless of content.

Another form of backfire occurs through isolation. As a strategy hardens, advice that challenges it is dismissed. Professionals who raise concerns are labeled compromised or uninformed. Support is sought only from sources that reinforce the chosen narrative. This narrowing of input reduces the chance of correction before consequences arise.

Forced strategies also backfire financially. Time spent pursuing ineffective approaches delays engagement with remedies that could mitigate loss. Costs accumulate — fees, penalties, interest — while attention remains fixed on arguments that do not alter outcomes. By the time reality intrudes, the margin for maneuver has shrunk.

There is also reputational risk. In legal settings, credibility matters. Parties who advance unsupported claims repeatedly may find their legitimate arguments discounted. Judges are human. Patterns influence perception. A party perceived as unwilling to engage with governing law faces an uphill battle even when raising valid points.

The discipline lies in assessing outcomes rather than intentions. If asserting a position does not change the behavior of lenders, taxing authorities, neighbors, or courts, repeating that assertion does not increase its force. It simply increases exposure. Recognizing when a strategy is being forced rather than applied is difficult precisely because commitment feels righteous. But if actions do not change conditions, repetition is not resolve; it is inertia.

Many property-related situations — boundary adjustments, administrative corrections, negotiated resolutions — improve through engagement. Introducing claims that challenge foundational authority often shuts down that engagement. Restraint preserves access to cooperative pathways that aggressive

strategies foreclose. Restraint also protects optionality. Once a claim is made formally, it becomes part of the record. It can influence how future actions are interpreted. Choosing not to act immediately keeps avenues open. It allows for recalibration as new information emerges. Forcing a patent strategy often stems from a desire for certainty in uncertain situations. That desire is understandable. Property represents security, identity, and continuity. Threats to it feel existential. But strategies must fit the environment in which they are deployed. When they do not, persistence amplifies harm. Avoiding backfire requires the willingness to revise assumptions in light of evidence. That willingness is not weakness. It is stewardship. When land patents are approached with restraint, they fulfill a valuable role. They inform understanding.

They clarify history. They contribute context. They do not become tools for confrontation or symbols of defiance. This balanced approach preserves their legitimacy and avoids distorting their significance.

Knowing When Restraint Is the Smarter Move

Knowing when restraint is the smarter move requires judgment developed through reflection rather than impulse. It involves asking not only "Can I do this?" but "What will this actually change?" and "What might it foreclose?" These questions are rarely answered by ideology. They are answered by experience, evidence, and careful thought.

Chapter 8 – Protecting Your Property the Smart Way

Practical Alternatives That Often Protect Property Better

Property protection is rarely achieved through a single decisive act. It is built through alignment—between documentation, behavior, and the legal environment in which ownership exists.

While land patents attract attention because of their historical weight, most practical protection comes from tools that operate squarely within the modern system.

These tools may feel less dramatic, but they are effective precisely because they engage with how property rights are actually recognized, defended, and enforced.

One of the most overlooked aspects of protection is predictability. Property is safest when other parties—buyers, lenders, insurers, courts—can predict how interests will be treated.

Tools that enhance predictability reduce friction. Tools that introduce ambiguity increase it.

Practical alternatives work not because they promise immunity, but because they reduce uncertainty.

Risk management is a central concept here. Ownership is exposed to risk from many directions: clerical error, undisclosed interests, procedural mistakes, competing claims, or changes in circumstance. No single document neutralizes all of these. Practical tools focus on identifying, allocating, and mitigating risk rather than denying its existence.

For example, maintaining clear, current records does not feel like protection in the abstract, but it becomes decisive when disputes arise. A homeowner who can produce a coherent, well-documented history of ownership stands on firmer ground than one who relies on theoretical arguments.

Courts reward clarity.

They penalize confusion.

Another effective alternative is proactive review. Periodically reviewing recorded documents, assessments, and public records allows issues to be addressed before they harden into disputes. Small discrepancies—an incorrect legal description, an unreleased interest, a misindexed document—are easier to resolve early.

Ignoring them does not make them disappear. It allows them to accumulate.
Negotiation is another underestimated protective tool.
Many property conflicts are resolved through agreement rather than adjudication.
Boundary adjustments, access arrangements, or administrative corrections often depend on cooperation. Approaches that frame property as absolute or adversarial tend to foreclose negotiation.

Practical strategies keep negotiation viable by operating within shared assumptions rather than challenging foundational authority.
Compliance also functions as protection. This does not mean passive acceptance of every obligation, but strategic engagement. Understanding what is required, what is optional, and what is contestable allows homeowners to choose their battles.
Contesting everything weakens credibility.
Choosing carefully strengthens it.
Practical protection also involves understanding leverage. Leverage arises from enforceable rights, not asserted ones. Rights grounded in statute, contract, or precedent can be exercised. Rights grounded in interpretation alone cannot. Effective tools increase leverage by aligning claims with recognized authority.

This alignment is why practical alternatives often outperform symbolic ones. They do not attempt to bypass the system; they use it. They work incrementally rather than dramatically. They may feel unsatisfying to those seeking certainty, but they deliver stability.

The goal of smart protection is not to eliminate risk, but to manage it intelligently. This requires accepting that ownership exists within constraints. Those constraints are not flaws. They are the conditions under which property can be bought, sold, financed, inherited, and defended.
As attention shifts from broad strategy to specific mechanisms, certain tools stand out for their consistent effectiveness.

Title Insurance, Corrective Instruments, and Documentation Hygiene

Among the most powerful yet misunderstood tools in property protection are those that operate quietly in the background.
They do not promise transformation.
They provide insulation.
Title insurance, corrective instruments, and documentation hygiene form a protective layer that absorbs shocks before they reach the surface.
Title insurance is often dismissed as a transactional formality. In reality, it is a risk allocation mechanism. It does not prevent defects from existing; it transfers the financial consequences of certain defects to an insurer.
This distinction matters. When a covered issue arises, the question is not whether ownership is philosophically sound, but whether the policy responds.

In many cases, it does. Standard title insurance policies follow forms developed by the American Land Title Association (ALTA).
An ALTA owner's policy covers, among other things, defects in title that were not known at issuance, claims from forged documents, undisclosed heirs, and certain errors in the public record.
An enhanced ALTA policy extends coverage to include post-policy risks such as encroachment by structures built after the policy date.
Lender's policies protect the mortgage holder's interest and are typically required by the lender as a condition of financing.
The one-time premium is paid at closing, and coverage lasts for as long as the insured — or their heirs — hold an interest in the property. No land patent, however old or however worded, provides comparable coverage.

The value of title insurance lies in its forward-looking function.
It acknowledges that not all risks can be identified in advance. Rather than pretending to eliminate uncertainty, it prepares for it. This preparation is tangible. It includes defense against claims, payment of losses, and resolution of disputes. These outcomes are concrete. They do not depend on interpretation.

Corrective instruments address a different category of vulnerability. They repair errors in the record. These errors are often mundane: a missing acknowledgment, a misdescribed parcel, an omitted signature. Yet their consequences can be significant.

Corrective instruments work because they speak the language of the recording system. They do not challenge authority; they satisfy requirements.

Many states have enacted curative statutes that automatically heal certain minor defects after a specified period.

For example, a deed that was notarized improperly may become immune from challenge after a number of years if no party has raised the defect.

These statutes vary by state and by the type of defect involved, but they share a common purpose: to promote stability in the recording system by preventing ancient technical flaws from derailing modern transactions.

When a curative statute applies, it accomplishes in the background what no patent claim could achieve through assertion.

Documentation hygiene is the discipline that keeps records usable. It involves maintaining copies, tracking changes, and ensuring consistency. Hygiene is preventative.

It does not respond to crisis; it reduces the likelihood of one. When disputes arise, well-maintained documentation accelerates resolution.

It reduces ambiguity.

It strengthens position.

For homeowners who want to take concrete steps, a reasonable documentation hygiene practice includes: keeping certified copies of the recorded deed and any title insurance policy in a secure location outside the home; reviewing the county assessor's records periodically to confirm that the legal description, assessed owner name, and property boundaries are accurate; verifying that any mortgage satisfaction or lien release has been properly recorded after a loan is paid off; checking whether any easements, covenants, or restrictions appear on the title that the owner was not aware of at purchase; confirming the status of mineral rights, if applicable, by examining the chain of title for any severance or reservation;

and maintaining a file that includes the survey, the title commitment, the closing documents, and all subsequent recorded instruments.

These steps are not dramatic, but they form the foundation on which all other protections rest.

What unites these tools is their orientation toward process.

They assume that property law is procedural and that outcomes depend on compliance. This assumption aligns with reality. Courts, insurers, and agencies operate through procedure. Tools that integrate smoothly into that process are effective.

These mechanisms also have a cumulative effect. Each one strengthens the others. Clear documentation supports insurance coverage. Corrective instruments improve record quality. Hygiene ensures continuity. Together, they create resilience.

Some homeowners resist these tools because they lack symbolic appeal.

They do not feel empowering.

They do not promise exemption. Yet empowerment in property matters comes from reliability, not rebellion. Knowing that defects can be addressed, disputes defended, and records clarified provides real security.

There is also a temporal aspect to these tools. They work over time. Their benefits accrue gradually. This contrasts with strategies that promise immediate transformation. The latter often disappoint because property systems do not transform quickly. They evolve.

Understanding the role of these mechanisms reframes what protection looks like. It becomes less about asserting status and more about maintaining integrity. Less about declarations and more about durability.

As ownership becomes more complex—through refinancing, inheritance, or development—the importance of these tools increases. Complexity amplifies risk. Structured mechanisms absorb it.

At some point, however, the limits of individual effort become apparent. Knowing where those limits lie is itself a form of protection.

When DIY Ends and Professional Help Begins

Self-education is a powerful asset. It allows homeowners to ask better questions, recognize weak advice, and avoid obvious pitfalls. Yet there is a point at which additional self-direction ceases to add value and begins to introduce risk.

Recognizing that point is not a failure of independence. It is an exercise of judgment.

Property law is layered not only in doctrine, but in procedure. Many outcomes hinge on timing, jurisdiction, and technical compliance. These variables are unforgiving.

Missing a deadline, filing in the wrong forum, or using incorrect language can negate otherwise valid positions. Professionals are trained to navigate these variables not because they are smarter, but because they are immersed in them.

One signal that professional help is warranted is when consequences become asymmetric. If the downside of error is large—loss of property, financial liability, prolonged litigation—the margin for experimentation narrows.

DIY approaches work best when mistakes are reversible. In high-stakes contexts, reversibility disappears.

Another signal arises when multiple systems intersect. Property issues often involve courts, recording offices, lenders, insurers, and regulatory bodies simultaneously.

Each system has its own rules.

Coordinating across them requires more than information; it requires experience.

Professionals function as translators between systems.

Without that translation, misalignment is common.

There is also a cognitive limit to self-representation. Individuals are deeply invested in their own outcomes. That investment can cloud judgment. Professionals provide distance. They are less attached to narratives and more focused on outcomes. This detachment is not indifference; it is functional clarity.

Choosing professional help does not mean surrendering control. It means reallocating it. The homeowner remains the decision-maker. The professional becomes an instrument.

The relationship works best when roles are clear: the homeowner sets objectives; the professional navigates execution. Finding the right professional begins with identifying the type of expertise needed.

A general practitioner may not have the depth required for complex title issues, mineral rights disputes, or adverse possession claims.

Homeowners should seek a licensed attorney who concentrates in real estate or property law within the relevant state.

Resources for locating qualified counsel include the state bar association's lawyer referral service, the American College of Real Estate Lawyers (ACREL), and directories such as martindale.com. For title-specific questions, a title company or title agent can often provide guidance, and many title insurers offer underwriting counsel who can evaluate unusual situations.

When mineral rights are involved, particularly in western states, a landman or mineral rights attorney with local experience is often essential. The initial consultation — which many attorneys offer at low or no cost — can clarify whether professional involvement is needed and, if so, what form it should take.

Another benefit of professional involvement is accountability. Advice carries weight when it is tied to standards, licensing, and liability. This accountability filters out many unsupported claims that circulate freely online. It also provides recourse when mistakes occur.

The transition from DIY to professional engagement is often framed as a loss of autonomy. In practice, it often restores it. It replaces guesswork with informed choice. It reduces the emotional burden of uncertainty.

Knowing when to seek help is not about humility alone. It is about efficiency. Time spent pursuing ineffective strategies is time not spent resolving issues. Professionals compress timelines by applying established pathways rather than exploring speculative ones.

There is also a protective function in signaling seriousness.

Courts and agencies respond differently when parties are represented competently. Filings are taken more seriously. Communications are clearer. Outcomes become more predictable.

The boundary between DIY and professional assistance is not fixed. It shifts with circumstance. What matters is not where the boundary lies, but whether it is recognized.
Smart property protection involves assembling the right mix of understanding, tools, and assistance. It avoids the extremes of blind delegation and rigid self-reliance. It adapts as conditions change.

Making a Responsible, Informed Decision About Your Property

At the end of any serious inquiry into property rights, documentation, and protection, one question remains unavoidable: *what should I actually do?* This question is deceptively simple.
It carries weight not because the answer is elusive, but because the consequences of acting—or not acting—are real.
Making a responsible, informed decision about property ownership is not about choosing the most compelling theory. It is about choosing a course of action that aligns understanding, risk tolerance, and long-term objectives within the system that governs outcomes.

Responsibility in property decisions begins with recognizing that ownership is not a static achievement. It is an ongoing condition that requires attention, maintenance, and judgment. Documents do not exist in isolation. Decisions do not exist without context. Every choice interacts with time, law, and other actors. Acting responsibly means accounting for those interactions rather than pretending they can be bypassed.

An informed decision is not one that eliminates uncertainty. Such a decision does not exist. It is one that acknowledges uncertainty and responds to it proportionally. This is where many homeowners struggle. The desire for certainty pushes them toward absolute claims, definitive solutions, and binary thinking. Responsible decision-making resists that impulse. It accepts that property ownership involves tradeoffs and that protecting one interest may expose another.
One of the most important elements of informed decision-making is clarity about objectives. Protecting property can mean different things depending on circumstance. For some, it means ensuring marketability for future sale.

For others, it means preserving family continuity. For others still, it means minimizing exposure to dispute or enforcement. These goals are not interchangeable.

Strategies that advance one may undermine another. Without clarity about priorities, decisions become reactive rather than strategic.

Risk tolerance plays an equally central role.

Every property decision carries risk, whether visible or hidden.

Some risks are financial, others procedural, others reputational. Responsible decision-making involves identifying which risks are acceptable and which are not.

This requires honesty. It is not enough to know what one *wants* to be true.

One must assess what one is prepared to absorb if things do not go as planned.

Information must be weighed, not collected endlessly.

There is a point at which additional research ceases to improve decisions and begins to reinforce preexisting beliefs. Informed decision-making recognizes diminishing returns. It values synthesis over accumulation.

Understanding improves when information is integrated into a coherent framework rather than stacked endlessly.

Another critical component is distinguishing between empowerment and exposure. Some actions feel empowering because they assert control.

Filing documents, making declarations, or adopting strong positions can provide psychological relief. Yet empowerment that increases exposure is illusory. Responsible decisions prioritize outcomes over emotions.

They ask not "Does this feel decisive?" but "Does this improve my position if challenged?"

Long-term thinking is essential here. Property decisions rarely resolve themselves quickly.

They unfold over years, sometimes generations. Choices that appear advantageous in the short term can create complications later. Responsible decision-making considers durability. It asks how a decision will age, how it will be interpreted by others, and how it will affect those who come after.

This forward-looking perspective often tempers dramatic action. It favors approaches that preserve flexibility, maintain credibility, and keep options open.

It avoids strategies that lock the owner into positions that may become difficult to defend or reverse. Restraint, in this sense, is not indecision. It is preservation of maneuverability.

Another hallmark of responsible decision-making is openness to adjustment.

New information, changing circumstances, or unexpected outcomes may require course correction. Decisions that are framed as irrevocable truths resist adaptation. Decisions framed as provisional strategies adapt more easily. Property systems reward adaptability because they themselves evolve.

It is also important to recognize that responsibility includes the impact of decisions on others. Property ownership exists within a social and legal fabric. Neighbors, heirs, lenders, and communities are affected by how property is managed. Decisions that ignore these relationships often generate conflict. Responsible decisions anticipate interaction rather than denial.

Professional input, when sought thoughtfully, contributes to informed choice. Not because professionals possess absolute answers, but because they bring perspective shaped by experience. They can identify blind spots, test assumptions, and clarify consequences. Responsible decision-making uses expertise as a resource, not as a substitute for judgment.

Ultimately, making a responsible, informed decision about property is an exercise in balance. It balances confidence with caution, autonomy with engagement, history with present reality. It avoids extremes. It does not chase certainty at the expense of stability, nor does it retreat into passivity.

The most secure property owners are not those who believe they have discovered a hidden key. They are those who understand how the system works, where its limits lie, and how to operate within it intelligently. Their decisions are quieter. They attract less attention. They endure. For the reader who has reached this point and wants to translate understanding into action, the following steps offer a starting place.

First, visit the county recorder's office or its online portal and obtain a copy of the most recent recorded deed for the property. Confirm that the legal description, owner names, and any referenced encumbrances are accurate.

Second, if the property is in a public-domain state, search the BLM-GLO Records database at glorecords.blm.gov to locate the original federal patent — not as a legal weapon, but as a matter of historical orientation.

Third, review any existing title insurance policy to understand what it covers and what it excludes.

Fourth, if any irregularities, unresolved liens, or unclear interests are discovered, consult a licensed real estate attorney in the state where the property is located before taking any action.

Fifth, refer to the Glossary and Appendices at the end of this book for definitions, statutory references, case law summaries, and research resources that support further independent inquiry.

Conclusion – Clarity Is the Real Advantage

Understanding Limits as a Form of Control

Property ownership is often framed as a quest for maximum authority.
The language surrounding it is filled with words like freedom, sovereignty, and absolute rights. Yet, after moving carefully through the realities of modern property law, a different picture emerges. Control does not come from denying limits. It comes from understanding them.

Limits are not signs of weakness. They are the boundaries within which decisions gain meaning.
A homeowner who understands where authority begins and ends is far less vulnerable than one who believes authority can be expanded through assertion alone.
Knowing what a document can do—and what it cannot—prevents misplaced confidence and wasted effort. It replaces illusion with orientation.
This kind of understanding changes posture.
Instead of pushing against the system blindly, the homeowner navigates within it deliberately.
Instead of reacting to perceived threats, they assess actual exposure.
Instead of seeking total insulation, they manage risk intelligently.
These shifts are subtle, but their effects are profound.

Clarity about limits also restores agency. When everything is framed as hidden, corrupt, or illegitimate, the individual is left with only two options: submission or rebellion.
Neither produces stability. Understanding limits introduces a third option: informed participation. That participation does not require agreement with every rule, but it does require recognition of how outcomes are determined.
Control grounded in clarity is quieter than control grounded in defiance. It does not announce itself. It does not rely on symbolic acts. It shows itself in consistency, preparedness, and proportion. This form of control may not satisfy the desire for certainty, but it sustains ownership over time.

Long-Term Thinking vs Short-Term Promises

One of the recurring themes throughout this guide has been the tension between immediacy and durability.
Many claims surrounding land patents promise quick resolution. They suggest that a single insight or filing can resolve complex problems.
These promises are appealing precisely because they compress effort and uncertainty into a moment of revelation.

Property law does not operate on revelation. It operates on accumulation. Rights are built through sequences of compliant actions. Protection emerges from alignment over time. Problems are rarely solved instantly; they are managed progressively.

Long-term thinking accepts this pace. It recognizes that ownership is not defended once, but continuously.
Decisions made today shape options years later. Records created now will be interpreted by people who do not share the current context. Actions taken under pressure may outlive the circumstances that motivated them.
Short-term promises often ignore this temporal dimension.
They focus on immediate relief rather than lasting position. When they fail, they leave behind confusion, damaged credibility, and fewer options.
Long-term thinking, by contrast, prioritizes reversibility, flexibility, and resilience.
This does not mean avoiding decisive action. It means choosing actions that age well. It means favoring strategies that remain defensible as circumstances change. It means recognizing that the absence of drama is often a sign of sound judgment.

Homeowners who think long-term tend to ask different questions. Not "What can I assert?" but "What will still make sense if this is challenged?" Not "How do I bypass this?" but "How do I reduce exposure?" These questions lead to different decisions—and different outcomes.

Acting Responsibly as a Property Owner

Responsibility in property ownership is not about compliance for its own sake. It is about stewardship.
Property represents shelter, value, continuity, and often family history.
Acting responsibly means protecting those interests not just from external threats, but from internal misjudgment.
Responsible ownership resists extremes.
It avoids both blind trust and reflexive distrust.
It does not assume the system is perfect, but it also does not pretend it can be ignored.
It works within reality rather than against it.
This responsibility extends beyond the individual.
Property decisions affect spouses, children, heirs, neighbors, and communities.
Choices made in pursuit of personal certainty can impose costs on others.
Responsible ownership considers those ripple effects.

It also involves humility.
No guide, no document, no strategy eliminates the need for judgment. Situations differ.
Laws change. Context matters. Responsibility lies in remaining attentive rather than clinging to fixed answers.

The purpose of this book has not been to provide a doctrine, an identity, or a shortcut. It has been to offer orientation. To replace confusion with proportion.
To separate what is historically meaningful from what is legally operative. To help homeowners evaluate relevance rather than inherit belief.

Clarity does not promise immunity. It promises perspective. That perspective allows for better decisions, fewer regrets, and stronger positioning when challenges arise.

The Glossary, statutory references, case law summaries, and research resources that follow in the Appendices are provided so that this perspective can be extended through independent inquiry. They are starting points, not endpoints.

In a landscape crowded with loud claims and absolute answers, clarity is the real advantage.

It does not shout.

It does not provoke.

It endures.

Glossary of Key Terms

The following definitions are provided for reference throughout this book. They reflect standard legal usage as applied in U.S. property law. Because state laws vary, readers should verify how specific terms are defined in their own jurisdiction.

Adverse Possession. A doctrine under which a person who occupies land continuously, openly, exclusively, and without permission for a period defined by state statute (typically 5 to 21 years) may acquire legal title to that land, even without a deed.
Allodial Title. A theoretical concept of ownership free from all obligations to a sovereign. It has no operative legal meaning in modern U.S. property law. All private property is subject to taxation, eminent domain, police power, and escheat.
Bundle of Rights. The collection of individual rights associated with property ownership, including the rights to use, exclude, transfer, encumber, and enjoy. Each right can be separated, limited, or conveyed independently.
Chain of Title. The sequential record of transfers, encumbrances, and other interests affecting a parcel of land, from the original conveyance (often a land patent or grant) through the current owner.
Cloud on Title. Any claim, lien, encumbrance, or defect that could impair the marketability or validity of a property title.
Conveyance. The transfer of a legal interest in real property from one party to another, typically through a deed.
Curative Statute. A state law that automatically corrects certain minor title defects (such as defective acknowledgments) after a specified period, promoting stability in the recording system.
Deed. A written instrument that transfers an interest in real property. Principal types include general warranty deed, special warranty deed, quitclaim deed, and bargain and sale deed.
Easement. A nonpossessory right to use another person's land for a limited purpose, such as access, drainage, or utility installation. Easements may be created by express grant, necessity, prescription, or implication.
Eminent Domain. The government's power to take private property for public use upon payment of just compensation, as required by the Fifth Amendment to the U.S. Constitution.
Encumbrance. Any right, interest, or claim that attaches to a property and may diminish its value or restrict its use, including liens, easements, mortgages, and restrictive covenants.
Escheat. The reversion of property to the state when the owner dies without heirs or a valid will.

Fee Simple. The most complete form of private ownership recognized in U.S. law. A fee simple estate is of potentially infinite duration and is subject only to the four governmental powers: taxation, eminent domain, police power, and escheat.

General Land Office (GLO). The federal agency created by Congress in 1812 (2 Stat. 716) to administer the disposition of public lands. In 1946, the GLO was merged with the Grazing Service to form the Bureau of Land Management (BLM).

Homestead Act. Federal legislation enacted in 1862 (12 Stat. 392) that granted 160 acres of public land to settlers who resided on and cultivated the land for five years. Repealed by FLPMA in 1976, with an exception for Alaska that continued until 1986.

Land Patent. A legal instrument (letters patent) by which a sovereign authority — typically the federal or state government — conveys public land into private ownership. It constitutes the root of title in the chain of ownership.

Lien. A legal claim against property that secures the payment of a debt or obligation. Types include mortgage liens, tax liens, mechanic's liens, and judgment liens.

Lis Pendens. A recorded notice indicating that a lawsuit affecting title to or possession of a specific property is pending.

Marketable Title. Title to property that is reasonably free from defects, encumbrances, and litigation risk, such that a prudent buyer would accept it and a title insurer would insure it without unusual exceptions.

Marketable Title Act. A state statute that limits how far back in time a title search must extend (typically 30–40 years), extinguishing most interests not preserved by re-recording within the statutory period. Enacted in at least 17 states.

Mineral Rights. Rights to extract subsurface minerals (oil, gas, coal, metals) from a property. Mineral rights can be severed from surface rights and conveyed or reserved separately. The mineral estate is generally considered the dominant estate.

Police Power. The authority of state and local government to regulate private property for the public health,safety, morals, and general welfare. Zoning, building codes, and environmental regulations derive from police power.

Prior Appropriation. The water rights doctrine followed in most western states, under which the first person to divert water and put it to beneficial use acquires the superior right, regardless of proximity to the water source. Contrasted with the riparian rights doctrine of eastern states.

Public Domain. Land owned by the federal government that has not been transferred into private ownership or reserved for a specific governmental purpose.

Public Land Survey System (PLSS). The rectangular survey system used in 30 public-domain states to describe land by reference to principal meridians, baselines, townships, ranges, and sections.
Quiet Title Action. A lawsuit filed to establish ownership of real property and to remove any clouds on the title. Federal quiet title actions against the United States are governed by 28 U.S.C. § 2409a.
Quitclaim Deed. A deed that conveys whatever interest the grantor may hold in the property, without any warranty as to the validity or extent of that interest.
Recording. The act of filing a document in the county recorder's (or register of deeds') office to provide public notice of an interest in real property. Recording does not create rights; it establishes priority and protects against subsequent claims.
Root of Title. The earliest document in the chain of title from which marketable title can be traced. In states with marketable title acts, the root of title is typically a transaction recorded at least 30–40 years ago.
Severed Estate. A condition in which different aspects of ownership (surface, minerals, water) have been separated and are held by different parties. Common in western states where patents reserved mineral rights to the government.
Slander of Title. A tort consisting of a false statement, made with malice, about another party's ownership of property, which causes actual financial damage. Recording baseless claims against a property can give rise to slander of title liability.
Sovereign Citizen. A pseudolegal movement whose adherents claim immunity from governmental authority on the basis of theories that have been rejected consistently by courts at every level. Land patent claims are frequently associated with sovereign citizen ideology.
Supremacy Clause. Article VI, Clause 2 of the U.S. Constitution, which provides that federal law is the supreme law of the land when it conflicts with state law. A land patent does not create an ongoing federal regulatory domain that triggers the Supremacy Clause.
Takings Clause. The provision of the Fifth Amendment prohibiting the government from taking private property for public use without just compensation. Regulatory takings doctrine, established in Pennsylvania Coal Co. v. Mahon, 260 U.S. 393 (1922), extends this protection to regulations that go too far in restricting property use.
Title Insurance. An insurance policy that protects the insured (owner or lender) against losses arising from defects in the title to real property. Standard policies follow forms issued by the American Land Title Association (ALTA).
Title Search. An examination of public records to determine the current state of title to a property, including the identity of the owner, any encumbrances, and any defects in the chain of title.

Transfer-on-Death Deed (TODD). A deed that transfers property to a named beneficiary upon the owner's death, avoiding probate. Authorized in approximately 30 states. Revocable during the owner's lifetime.

Township and Range. The grid-based system of legal descriptions used in the Public Land Survey System. A township is a 6-mile-by-6-mile square, divided into 36 sections of approximately 640 acres each.

Zoning. The division of a municipality into districts with regulations governing the use, height, density, and placement of structures. Upheld as constitutional in Village of Euclid v. Ambler Realty Co., 272 U.S. 365 (1926).

Appendix A — Key Statutory and Constitutional References

The following references are provided to support independent research. They are not exhaustive and do not constitute a survey of all applicable law. State-specific statutes must be verified in the relevant jurisdiction.

U.S. Constitution

• Article IV, Section 3, Clause 2 (Property Clause) — Congressional power to dispose of public lands

• Article VI, Clause 2 (Supremacy Clause) — Federal law supreme when conflicting with state law

• Fifth Amendment (Takings Clause) — Private property not taken without just compensation

• Tenth Amendment — Powers not delegated to federal government reserved to states

• Fourteenth Amendment (Due Process / Equal Protection) — Applicable to state regulation of property

Federal Statutes

• General Land Office Act, April 25, 1812, 2 Stat. 716 — Created the GLO to manage public land disposition

• Land Ordinance of 1785 — Established the rectangular survey system for public lands

• Northwest Ordinance of 1787 — Provided framework for territorial governance and land disposition

• Homestead Act of 1862, 12 Stat. 392 — Authorized 160-acre homesteads on public domain

• Mining Law of 1872, 30 U.S.C. §§ 22–54 — Authorized mineral exploration and patents on public lands

• Desert Land Act of 1877, 43 U.S.C. § 321 et seq. — Encouraged irrigation-based settlement of arid lands

• Timber Culture Act of 1873 — Encouraged tree planting on public lands (repealed 1891)

• Stock Raising Homestead Act of 1916, Section 9 — Reserved all mineral rights to the United States in patents issued under this act

• Federal Land Policy and Management Act (FLPMA), 1976, 43 U.S.C. § 1701 et seq. — Declared national policy of retaining public lands in federal ownership; ended general homestead-type patenting

- Quiet Title Act of 1972, 28 U.S.C. § 2409a — Allows private parties to bring title actions against the United States
- 11 U.S.C. § 362 — Automatic stay in bankruptcy proceedings
- Federal Rule of Civil Procedure 11 — Sanctions for frivolous filings

State Statute Examples

- Florida — F.S. Ch. 712 (Marketable Record Title Act, 30-year root of title)
- California — Civ. Code § 880.020 et seq. (Marketable Title); Penal Code § 115 (filing false instruments, felony)
- Oklahoma — 12 O.S. § 1141 (Quiet Title Actions)
- North Carolina — Ch. 47B (Marketable Title Act, 30-year period)
- Colorado — C.R.S. § 38-35-109 (civil remedies against fraudulent lien filings)
- Texas — Natural Resources Code (General Land Office records and grants)
- Michigan — M.C.L. Ch. 565 (recording and conveyancing); submerged land patent case law
- Ohio — R.C. Ch. 5301 (Marketable Title Act, 40-year period)

Appendix B — Key Court Decisions

The following cases are cited throughout this book and represent the most relevant judicial authorities on the interaction between land patents and modern property law. Citations are to the official reporters. Full texts are available through resources listed in Appendix C.

Roads v. Symmes, 1 Ohio 281, 314 (1824)
Established that a patent is "the consummation of the title," not its foundation; once issued, the government's legal power over the land terminates.

Wilcox v. Jackson, 38 U.S. (13 Pet.) 498 (1839)
The foundational Supreme Court decision on land patents. Held that once title passes under federal law, the property becomes subject to state legislation like all other property within the state.

Beard v. Federy, 70 U.S. (3 Wall.) 478 (1865)
Described the operation of a land patent as essentially that of a quitclaim — a conveyance of whatever interest the United States possessed in the land.

McCulloch v. Maryland, 17 U.S. (4 Wheat.) 316 (1819)
Affirmed the fundamental nature of the taxing power and the supremacy of federal law within its enumerated scope.

Pennsylvania Coal Co. v. Mahon, 260 U.S. 393 (1922)
Established the regulatory takings doctrine: a government regulation that "goes too far" in restricting property use constitutes a taking requiring just compensation.

Village of Euclid v. Ambler Realty Co., 272 U.S. 365 (1926)
Upheld comprehensive municipal zoning as a valid exercise of the state's police power under the Fourteenth Amendment. Never overturned.

Kaiser Aetna v. United States, 444 U.S. 164 (1979)
Identified the right to exclude others as "one of the most essential sticks in the bundle of rights that are commonly characterized as property."

Summa Corp. v. California, 466 U.S. 198 (1984)
Confirmed that a federal land patent does not prevent a state from exercising regulatory authority over the conveyed land.
BFP v. Resolution Trust Corp., 511 U.S. 531 (1994)
Held that a foreclosure sale conducted in compliance with state law is presumptively valid and not subject to avoidance as a fraudulent transfer.
Kelo v. City of New London, 545 U.S. 469 (2005)
Held that economic development can constitute "public use" sufficient to support the exercise of eminent domain under the Fifth Amendment.
United States v. Benabe, 654 F.3d 753 (7th Cir. 2011)
Rejected sovereign citizen jurisdictional arguments: "Regardless of an individual's claimed status of descent ...that person is not beyond the jurisdiction of the courts."
Meads v. Meads, 2012 ABQB 571 (Alberta, Canada)
Comprehensive judicial taxonomy of pseudolegal arguments including land patent theories, sovereign citizen claims, and "strawman" doctrines. Widely cited in American legal scholarship.
Sheetz v. County of El Dorado, California (2024)
Held that the Takings Clause applies equally to legislatively imposed and administratively imposed conditions on land-use permits.

Appendix C — Research Resources and Bibliography

Official Databases and Online Resources
BLM General Land Office Records — glorecords.blm.gov
Free online access to over five million federal land patent records (1820–present), survey plats, master title plats, and field notes. Covers the 30 public-domain states only.
National Archives — Land Records — archives.gov/research/land
Land entry case files (Record Group 49) containing patent application papers, affidavits, and compliance documents. Held at the National Archives Building in Washington, D.C.
Texas General Land Office — glo.texas.gov
Searchable Land Grant Database covering Spanish, Mexican, and Republic of Texas grants. Texas is a state-land state; its records are not in the BLM system.
Pennsylvania State Archives — phmc.state.pa.us
Patent index images from 1684 to 1957 for land conveyed through William Penn's proprietary grants and subsequent state patents.
FamilySearchLand Patent Search Guide
familysearch.org/wiki/Land_Patent_Search
Comprehensive guide to searching federal land patent records for genealogical and historical research purposes.
Cornell Legal Information Institute — law.cornell.edu
Full text of the U.S. Code, Constitution, Federal Rules, and Supreme Court opinions. Free and publicly accessible.
Justia U.S. Supreme Court Center — supreme.justia.com
Searchable database of U.S. Supreme Court decisions organized by topic, including property rights and land use.
American Land Title Association (ALTA) — alta.org
Industry standards, policy forms, and educational resources related to title insurance and the title examination process.

State Bar Association Lawyer Referral Services
Each state bar association operates a referral service that can connect homeowners with licensed attorneys who practice real estate law in the relevant jurisdiction.

Bibliography

• Wright & Muth, "Land Patents: Are They an Escape from Foreclosure?," 36 Drake Law Review 561–583 (1988). The leading academic article analyzing land patent claims in the context of modern property law.

• Gates, Paul W., History of Public Land Law Development (1968). The definitive historical study of federal land disposition in the United States. Commissioned by the Public Land Law Review Commission.

• Friedman, Lawrence M., A History of American Law (4th ed., Oxford University Press, 2019). Comprehensive history of the American legal system, including extensive treatment of property law's development.

• Dukeminier, Krier, Alexander, Schill & Strahilevitz, Property (Aspen Casebook Series, 9th ed., 2018). The standard law school casebook on property law, covering estates, conveyancing, recording, and land use.

• Palomar, Joyce, Patton and Palomar on Land Titles (3rd ed., West). A practitioner-oriented treatise on title examination, recording, and title insurance.

• Black's Law Dictionary (12th ed., Thomson Reuters, 2024). The authoritative dictionary of legal terms used by courts, practitioners, and scholars throughout the United States.

• Bureau of Land Management, Historical Highlights of Public Land Management. Government publication providing a chronological overview of federal land policy from the colonial era to the present.

Appendix D — Key Differences Among the States

Property law varies significantly from state to state. The tables below identify major areas of variation relevant to topics discussed in this book. They are intended as orientation, not as a substitute for state-specific legal research.

D.1 — Land Origin: Public-Domain States vs State-Land States

Public-Domain States (30): Alabama, Alaska, Arizona, Arkansas, California, Colorado, Florida, Idaho, Illinois, Indiana, Iowa, Kansas, Louisiana, Michigan, Minnesota, Mississippi, Missouri, Montana, Nebraska, Nevada, New Mexico, North Dakota, Ohio, Oklahoma, Oregon, South Dakota, Utah, Washington, Wisconsin, Wyoming. Federal land patent records are searchable at glorecords.blm.gov.

State-Land States (20): Connecticut, Delaware, Georgia, Maryland, Massachusetts, New Hampshire, New Jersey, New York, North Carolina, Pennsylvania, Rhode Island, South Carolina, Virginia, Vermont, Kentucky, Tennessee, Maine, West Virginia, Texas, Hawaii. Land origin records are held at state archives or state land offices, not at the BLM.

D.2 — Recording Statutes

System	Rule	States
Race	First to record prevails, regardless of notice	NC, LA (in part)
Notice	Last good-faith purchaser without notice prevails	AL, AZ, CT, FL, IL, KS, MA, ME, MO, NH, NM, OK, RI, SC, TN, TX, VT, WV
Race-Notice	Must lack notice AND record first	AK, AR, CA, CO, DC, GA, HI, ID, IN, IA, KY, MD, MI, MN, MS, MT, NE, NV, NJ, NY, ND, OH, OR, PA, SD, UT, VA, WA, WI, WY

D.3 — Marketable Title Acts

Enacted in at least 17 states: Connecticut, Florida, Illinois, Indiana, Iowa, Kansas, Michigan, Minnesota, Nebraska, North Carolina, North Dakota, Ohio, Oklahoma, South Dakota, Utah, Vermont, and Wyoming. Typical lookback period: 30–40 years. Effect: most interests not preserved by re-recording within the statutory period are extinguished. In these states, the original land patent is almost never examined in a routine title search.

D.4 — Mortgage Theory: Title vs Lien vs Intermediary

Title Theory (~20 states, e.g., GA, MA, MD, ME, NC, NH, VA): The lender holds legal title to the property during the term of the loan. Lien Theory (~30 states, e.g., CA, NY, FL, TX, IL, OH, PA, WA): The borrower retains title; the lender holds only a security interest. Intermediary Theory (e.g., NJ, OH in some contexts): The lender acquires title only upon borrower default. The distinction primarily affects foreclosure procedures and the borrower's rights during repayment.

D.5 — Adverse Possession: Statutory Periods

Periods range from 5 years (California, with tax payment) to 21 years (Pennsylvania). Common periods include: 7 years (FL), 10 years (IN, MT, NY, TX with various conditions), 15 years (MI, MN, NJ, OH, VA), 20 years (CT, IL, MA, WI). Some states require payment of property taxes during the adverse possession period (e.g., TX, CA); others do not. All states require that possession be actual, open, notorious, exclusive, hostile, and continuous for the full statutory period. State-specific requirements must be verified.

D.6 — Mineral Rights and Severed Estates

In western public-domain states, many land patents reserved mineral rights to the United States, particularly under the Stock Raising Homestead Act of 1916. When those minerals were later disposed of, a severed mineral estate was created. In Texas, the General Land Office manages state-owned mineral interests separately. In eastern states, mineral rights generally pass with the surface unless expressly reserved or severed in the chain of title. Several states have enacted Dormant Mineral Acts or similar statutes that allow surface owners to extinguish long-unused mineral interests through a notice-and-recording procedure. The specific status of mineral rights for any property must be determined by examining the full chain of title, beginning with the original patent or grant.

NOTES

www.ingramcontent.com/pod-product-compliance
Lightning Source LLC
LaVergne TN
LVHW022116200926
848481LV00003B/1179
* 9 7 9 8 8 9 8 4 3 3 3 5 2 *